GOSSIP BOYS

THE UNAUTHORISED BIOGRAPHY OF
CHACE CRAWFORD

LIZ KAYE

10 9 8 7 6 5 4 3 2 1

First published in the UK in 2011 by Virgin Books,
an imprint of Ebury Publishing
A Random House Group Company

Copyright © Liz Kaye

Chace cover image © Stephan Cardinale/People Avenue/Corbis

www.randomhouse.co.uk

Addresses for companies within The Random House Group Limited can be
found at www.randomhouse.co.uk/offices.htm

The Random House Group Limited Reg. No. 954009

A CIP catalogue record for this book is available from the British Library

ISBN: 978075340282

The Random House Group Limited supports The Forest Stewardship
Council (FSC®), the leading international forest certification organisation.
Our books carrying the FSC label are printed on FSC® certified paper. FSC is
the only forest certification scheme endorsed by the leading environmental
organisations, including Greenpeace. Our paper procurement policy can be
found at www.randomhouse.co.uk/environment

MIX
Paper from
responsible sources
FSC® C016897

Printed and bound by CPI Group (UK) Ltd, Croydon, CR0 4YY
To buy books by your favourite authors and register for offers visit
www.randomhouse.co.uk

Contents

Chapter 1: Early Life 7

Chapter 2: Decision Time 17

Chapter 3: Warlocks and Worries 29

Chapter 4: Gossip Girl 39

Chapter 5: Loaded With Fame 59

Chapter 6: 'Have You Met My Friend Chuck?' 75

Chapter 7: The Celebrity Circus 85

Chapter 8: Not Exactly The West Side 101

Chapter 9: Dark Times 111

Chapter 10: He's Just Getting Started 119

CHAPTER 1

Early Life

SEVENTEEN:

Fill in the blank: When I was 17, I was _____

CHACE CRAWFORD:

'Ignorant. No, I was ... very fortunate. No, I was ... spunky. I was ... rebellious. Black sheep of the family. Any one of those. I was ... happy to graduate from high school. I was ... in Texas. I was ... loving life at 17. It was easier, less complicated. I was ... simple. How 'bout that? I was just simple.

THE SIMPLE LIFE IS the very opposite of what Chace Crawford's character in *Gossip Girl* enjoys. Nate Archibald lives in the ultra-wealthy Upper East Side of Manhattan where his world is a whirlwind of parties, limousines, girls and complicated, turbulent relationships. In terms of emotional upheaval, Nate's life is almost the exact opposite of the childhood that Chace Crawford was lucky enough to experience. Chace was born in Lubbock in the north-western corner of Texas, the birthplace of many prominent country musicians and basketball stars such as Craig Ehlo and Daniel Santiago, as well as football player Mason Crosby. Possibly its most famous resident was the 1950s rock and roll legend Buddy Holly!

However, when Chace was just a young boy, his family relocated 300 miles directly east past Fort Worth to the city of Plano, and so he spent much of his childhood in and around Dallas, a city he loves to this day. Notable Plano residents include legendary cyclist Lance Armstrong and golfer Fred Couples.

Chace was born on 18 July 1985 with a host of famous names: Nelson Mandela, astronaut John Glenn and billionaire entrepreneur Richard Branson. His full name is actually Christopher Chace Crawford, but he chooses to use his more distinctive middle moniker.

The Crawford family was very hard-working and were clearly fortunate to live in Plano – in 2005 the city was voted the 'Best Place to Live' in the western United States. And it's here that such well-known and distinctive American brands Pizza Hut, JC Penney and Dr Pepper are located, so perhaps their presence contributes to the area's affluence. It consistently ranks highly in the list of America's wealthiest cities (being rated the wealthiest in 2008) and in 2010 it won the equally enviable accolade as 'The Safest City to live in America'. Shades of Nate Archibald's own lifestyle perhaps? Chace himself seems acutely aware of his privileged upbringing and openly speaks of his gratitude: 'The best thing about [living in the South],' he told *Female First*, 'is the way I was raised. I'm so thankful for my background. I feel like I've got a good head on my shoulders and that my parents raised me right. I just love the people there in general in the South. It's a great atmosphere and a great place to actually live – so I'm really thankful for that.'

Chace's father Chris is a dermatologist while his mother Dana is a teacher. His parents had met at a young age ('it's a Southern thing!') and by the time his father was at med school, Chace's mum was expecting his younger sister Candice. According to Chace, a huge upside of starting their family this young is that his parents are still young themselves; he felt the full benefit of this when his acting career took off in his late teens and early twenties because his mum and dad encouraged and advised him through the firestorm of international fame and fortune without the distance of a generation gap.

Chace paints a lovely picture of a very close family sitting down to eat his mother's beautiful chicken and rice. 'My mom kept the household together, managed everything. We were her life.' The closeness of the Crawford family has remained even though their son is now a superstar actor – fast forward to 2011 and Chace is a very famous face on the TV, but without fail he still phones his parents every single day.

And yes, Chace's stunning looks were there from a very young age! His sister Candice is also fortunate in the looks department and has gone on to become a beauty queen. Chace himself has spoken about this familial beauty to blockbuster.co.uk: 'I'm blessed. I have a beautiful mother and beautiful father so I guess you could say I'm blessed with good genes.' He says his father never really bombarded him with skincare tips but there would often be family friends' girls in the kitchen where his dad would help them out with their teenage skincare worries. In later years, when Chace had become a famous TV star, he joked with reporters about how much his father's profession affected his looks: 'He would give me face wash, I had Botox age nine, that's when we started. And then just the occasional facelift.'

It wasn't all roses for Chace, however. He attended Ridgeview Elementary and it was here that his mum made him wear 'crazily' brief cut-off jeans. 'I suffered from it. But at least I learned quite early that there's no reason for men to wear shorts.' On a more serious note, when talking to *ES* magazine on a promotional trip to the UK in 2010, Chace shocked his many fans by revealing that he was diagnosed – incorrectly, in his opinion – with Attention Deficit Disorder or ADD. He was even prescribed a drug to alleviate the condition but this was something he would later feel was an overreaction: 'I don't think I am ADD. Now I'm much more interested in knowledge and learning. I watch a lot of documentaries and news, I have a hunger for that. As a kid, I was more interested in daydreaming and friends ... They used to really overprescribe that stuff ... Maybe it was good I took a little bit of medication, y'know? To help facilitate my schoolwork.' He admits that at times he would utilise his 'wild imagination' and draw 'masterpieces of the stupidest things!'

Not surprisingly Chace's good looks attracted a lot of female attention at school! He was relatively shy but very popular and as he grew older his confidence began to grow. His first kiss, at the age of 11, was in sixth grade when his class was on summer camp. All of his mates had girlfriends and he really liked one particular girl. Despite admitting that he was 'a very awkward kisser', he is warmly sentimental about this pre-teenage romance: '[My first kiss] was very picturesque on this cliff with my first girlfriend, Kiley. She was my best friend's twin sister. I'm actually good friends with her today!' When it came to Valentine's Day, Chace gave Kiley a home-made mixtape.

The Crawford family spent four years in Bloomington, Minnesota which is why there are hints of that region's accent in Chace's soft voice, rather than just a pure Texan drawl. From his early teens, Chace attended Trinity Christian Academy whose website states it 'is an independent co-educational school that offers a college preparatory curriculum within a Christian community committed to integrating Biblical faith and learning. The school desires to educate and develop the whole person for the glory of God by helping equip each student to grow in the grace and knowledge of

Jesus Christ, and to become a faithful disciple of Him.' The religious choice of school mirrored the Crawford family's values – Chace was raised as a Southern Baptist and they attended church regularly.

Fees to attend the school (as of 2011) can be as much as $16,000. The campus places a strong emphasis on sports with over fifty teams, including baseball, wrestling and football. Not surprisingly, perhaps, the school also has several fine arts courses such as visual arts, drama and choir.

The school was a relatively small establishment and when he was a star on *Gossip Girl*, Chace would often be asked how his own school days at a private campus compare to the very privileged life that the characters on the hit show enjoy: 'It's just different, I learnt about the bubble [though], a really small high school, that whole situation and the gossip, the smaller it gets the worse it is.'

Chace was a strong sportsman at high school and was said to particularly excel at golf with a handicap of six, which earned him a slot on the college team. In fact, he played so much golf that even the aroma of a neatly clipped green brings him out all sporty: 'When I smell freshly cut grass I get this air of competition,' he told reporter Lisa Ingrassia. 'It wakes me up, gets me going. It energises me in a certain way. It's liberating.' With this golfing background in mind, he once said, 'I was a nerd, quite awkward', yet he was also excellent at the more macho sport of American football, playing as quarterback.

Chace was also a talented artist and after he hit the big time with *Gossip Girl* he filled his bachelor's apartment with numerous stunning works of art and would spend hours going around the various art galleries in Chelsea Pier, New York. Back when he was a teenage boy, he worked primarily with watercolours, charcoal and pastels, though as an adult he tends to concentrate on sketching. It was during this time that he also developed quite a skill for photography, buying a 35mm camera and teaching himself the techniques required. He later credited this skill with helping his acting, as he said the techniques needed to compose a good photograph gave him a deeper understanding of the composition that a director has to achieve on set. 'Everything was so intriguing to me,' he told *Female First*, 'and I really fell in love with [art] you know. Art has now become a part of me, and a part of my life because it's so interesting.'

However, for the teenage Chace, there were also far more serious events around the corner, as he revealed in an interview with *Fabulous* magazine: 'I went to juvenile detention when I was 15. It was all over a little misunderstanding with a pellet gun! I accidentally hit somebody on a golf course so I went to the centre for the weekend. At the time my parents went ballistic, but it's a joke now.'

Looking back on those (relatively!) innocent days, Chace describes himself as quite a shy teenager prone to over-analysing situations, 'a bit over-zealous', as he puts it. Still, the usual teenage rites of passage seem to have been something he enjoyed: when he was 16 his father gave him a black Chevy

Tahoe truck in which he would 'basically drive around and wreck things'. Girls went hand in hand with his wheels. 'So much happened in it,' he later cheekily told *People* magazine, 'I can't even tell you how emotional it was to get rid of that truck!'

Chace has also detailed an 'awkward' phase in high school when he felt very much less than the local hunk – he had braces on his teeth for a year and then followed that up by having blond tips in his hair. 'That was my absolute low point,' he later laughed. Yet he was eventually voted 'Best Dressed' in his senior year of high school.

He says he wasn't bullied at school although there was a tradition that when every pupil reached the age of 16, they had to be beaten up by their 'mates' 16 times! 'You just had to take it. It did hurt – I didn't get cut, but I got some pretty good welts.'

One of his summer jobs at high school was working at Abercrombie & Fitch – which he hated! 'They play the same three CDs all day long. They play it so loud you can't even talk in the store and they blast the place with cologne, you can smell it from a block away. I was a greeter. I had to stand out front and time would drag on. I'd beg them to let me work on the cash register.' Interestingly, this job led to modelling work for their sibling store, Hollister, which aims their products at younger teens.

Chace's stunning good looks meant that his popularity with the girls in junior high continued with the girls at high school.

One of his first girlfriends was unfortunate enough to receive the worst brush-off that Chace would admit to – when he decided he wanted to split up, he left a note under her windscreen wiper! 'I felt like I could get everything out that way. I was only 14. I'll never do that again!' When he was older, he was talked into a blind date but it was a disaster and he swore never to do this again.

Overall, Chace has great memories of his time at Trinity, as he told the *Inquirer*: 'I actually had a great high school experience. My school was small so I got to know everybody.' Towards the end of his time there, two developments arose that would have a massive impact on Chace's future TV career. It was while he was in his senior year that Chace had his very first experience of acting. Before this, he'd often quoted famous movie lines around the house but only as a boyish bit of fun with no thoughts about a career. However, while at Trinity his drama teacher asked him if he would audition for a role in a production of *The Boyfriend*. Chace duly did – choosing to sing the National Anthem – and he won the part. At this stage, however, even winning this sought-after role did not incite in Chace a burning passion for the stage: 'It was a good little role and something about it was just fun, but it didn't even really trigger anything in me.' Qualifying this indifference a little more, he explained that he hadn't enjoyed the singing part of the musical (by his own admission he is 'not the best singer in the world'), but the acting side had interested him and it was probably this debut production that started the flicker of interest that would eventually lead him to *Gossip Girl*.

Also while attending Trinity (from where he graduated in 2003), Chace had begun some low-key modelling work, principally around Dallas – he later said he 'hated' this line of work as it didn't always pay too well and they treated the models 'like a piece of meat'. Some of these modelling snaps later appeared on the Internet after he had broken big in *Gossip Girl* and show him without a shirt and wearing a cowboy's tasselled leather jacket and ten-gallon hat, in a stereotypical 'beefcake' pose. His famous eyebrows were already very prominent, a feature later described as 'the greatest eyebrows this side of Zac Efron'. Chace himself has been less complimentary, saying, 'They're like Brillo pads! But I just kinda let 'em go. I don't like looking that clean.'

It was during his mid-to-late teens that Chace began a relationship that to this day is his longest with any girl, over three years. Somehow – in true Nate Archibald style! – he 'ended up dating one of her friends!' After this drama, Chace chose to stay resolutely single for some time to come, no wonder!

CHAPTER 2

Decision Time

AFTER HIS EVENTFUL HIGH school years, it was off to Malibu's Pepperdine University, an enviable place to study, situated as it is on an 830-acre campus overlooking the Pacific Ocean. As with Trinity, there was an emphasis on religion with the small Jesuit university proudly saying: 'It is the purpose of Pepperdine University to pursue the very highest academic standards within a context that celebrates and extends the spiritual and ethical ideals of the Christian faith.'

It is widely reported that Chace was a member of the Sigma Nu fraternity at Pepperdine, although their official website has no mention of him under their 'Famous Members' section (Harrison Ford was a member though!). Notable other entertainment alumni from Pepperdine include former Miss World, Lisa-Marie Kohrs, R&B star Montell Jordan, and George Schlatter, the Emmy-winning American television producer and director, best known for *Rowan and Martin's Laugh-In*.

It was at Pepperdine in his fraternity house that Chace had his first 'supernatural' experience when he saw a strange, ethereal figure that soon vanished. This left him with the view that ghosts and spirits definitely exist – a belief that in the future would prove to be remarkably appropriate for one of his first cinematic roles.

In another nod to his future role in *Gossip Girl*, many of the fellow pupils at Pepperdine were from very wealthy families: 'There were a lot of kids there whose families were very rich. The parents would be on private jets on business trips all the time and, although you could see they loved their kids, they weren't there.' Chace's course at Pepperdine was journalism, but he would switch majors twice because he was unsure of his career ambitions. Famous faces often admit they had no idea of an exact career path at first, but *always* knew they didn't want to conform; Chace is no exception: 'I never felt I would have a desk job,' he told *VMan*. 'I knew I had to fulfil my creative side, my creative needs.'

Consequently Chace kept chopping and changing his degree, with journalism, advertising, business and communication majors all being studied. 'Everyone else knew what they wanted to do. But not me – I was the lone wolf,' he once told *Teen Vogue*. With great honesty, he has since admitted to feeling genuinely 'confused' during this phase of his university studies and that he often worried about how his peer group all seemed to know what they wanted to do (he has since realised that this perception was 'complete bullshit'). One of the few activities that Chace definitely enjoyed – alongside more golf, football and other sports – was acting, which he had started doing at university as a hobby but became increasingly captivated by as the terms went by. Over time he realised that acting was where his passion actually lay; maybe, just maybe it could also be where his career was destined to take him?

With this exciting realisation, Chace became suddenly very focused indeed on his future. He started going to acting lessons most evenings and he was beginning to adore the idea of working in the profession. During this time, a friend suggested he contact a TV commercials agent. Hollywood legend has it that when the completely stunning Chace Crawford took his friend's advice and walked into the agent's office, the admirably visionary agent took one look at him and said, 'Welcome … Yes!'

A handful of adverts followed but Chace was always looking for serious acting opportunities. Perhaps not surprisingly, given his recent modelling work and incredible good looks, it wasn't long before Chace secured himself an acting agent too. The very first agent who interviewed him snapped him up and put Chace straight on his books. In his initial interview, it's rumoured that the agent asked him, 'Can you do improv?' to which the green-behind-the-ears Chace responded, 'What's improv?'

Once signed to the acting agent, Chace began studying theatrical techniques even more intensely and his fierce ambition and hard work soon reaped dividends. He found that the majority of acting class students weren't really focused and didn't apply themselves. By contrast, he felt there was no point being there at all unless he committed himself 100 per cent.

After just a year of his broadcast journalism major, his acting career looked like it was starting to take off. 'I was just only sure of what I didn't want to do,' he told Josh Clinton of *Prime Time Pulse*: 'I was young, I had a year ahead of everyone else in school … a friend of a friend put me through to [that] commercial agent and they agreed to work with me. That got the ball rolling for me, and [later] it all started to click for me in acting class.' He's also modestly said he 'sort of fell into a little acting during that time'. What is clear is that he was very driven – now he had found a career that he was passionate about, he was going to aim high and work hard. Signing to the agents was a brilliant start: 'Finding someone who will push you and believe in you, that's the first big step,' he later told *Wonderland* magazine, 'and I started getting really good feedback right away.'

He still wasn't convinced though; commuting between college and various short-notice auditions was proving to be practically very difficult and when his father asked him how things were going one day, Chace was totally honest. 'Listen, I'm half-assing both things, Dad,' he admitted. To his amazement, his dad told him to take some time out of school and go full-on for the acting life.

Encouraged in this fantastic way, Chace decided to take a semester off, principally to see if a sharper focus on acting might reap results. Rather than chide him for wasting his education, his very supportive parents were totally behind their son: 'It was a practical move,' his mother has since said, explaining that Chace had taken a career aptitude test that suggested he was best suited for a job in the performing arts. In later interviews Chace regularly references this aptitude test, so it must have had quite an effect on him.

However, like millions of aspiring actors before him, Chace had no income so he would make ends meet by working as a car valet, grinding out a meagre living parking vehicles at a seaside restaurant in Malibu. He's admitted to sometimes stealing his customer's chewing gum from their glove compartments and even declared that he wasn't even that good at the job anyway! One day the famous and notorious rap music mogul Suge Knight came in and Chace was so nervous that he asked a colleague to move Suge's car! Years later, when Chace was a hot Hollywood property, Wrigley's chewing gum heard the story of the illicit chewing-gum raids on customers' cars and sent him a load of free gum, saying that he didn't have to steal it from glove boxes any more!

Despite the very modest pay, Chace really enjoyed his time as a valet and later called it 'one of the best jobs I've ever had. I loved it.' The site was next to the beach and as a petrol-head he thoroughly enjoyed being around swanky cars all day. However, acting was his bug and he knew that valeting cars was only ever a way of putting food on the table. Luckily, Chace's first ever movie role was just around the corner ...

Like all aspiring actors, Chace was not in a position to pick and choose his roles as he would be able to in his post-*Gossip Girl* years. Although many fans think his first screen time came with the 2006 film, *Covenant* (more of which later), in fact his debut was some five months earlier, in a made-for-television film called *Long Lost Son*, originally broadcast in the summer of 2006.

The project was directed by Brian Trenchard-Smith, an English producer, director and actor who had made a name for himself with many films in the horror and action genres in Australia. His most notable successes were films such as *The Man from Hong Kong* and the award-winning *The Quest*.

The film was made by Lifetime Television, an American network that focuses on movies, sitcoms and dramas aimed at the female viewer, most often with a woman in the lead role (until 2005, the channel's tag line was 'Television for Women'). Comedians have been known to refer to Lifetime as 'The Estrogen Channel' or 'Wifetime'. So it's perhaps not entirely surprising that it was on just such a channel that the astoundingly handsome Chace Crawford got his first break!

Long Lost Son opens with Kristen, a doting young mother, played by Gabrielle Anwar (perhaps best known for her tango with Al Pacino in *Scent of a Woman*) lying next to her young son on the floor, painting, chatting and laughing together. Their joy is interrupted by the arrival of her estranged husband; their troubled marriage is heading for a divorce and while living apart the son starts to see his father only once a month at weekends. On one visit, despite asking her ex not to take their son out sailing as a dangerous storm is approaching, he does exactly that, which leads to the apparent disaster that underpins the entire movie.

Father and son head out on their boat the *Ocean Dreamer* in a foul storm; not long after they set off however, a radio signal reports they are having difficulties and have lost a mast. Soon after that, the ship is reported 'Lost at Sea' with no sign of any survivors.

Retreating into a shell of grief and despair, Kristen slowly rebuilds her life and eventually remarries. However, while unwittingly watching a friend's holiday video 14 years after the disaster, Kristen sees a man in the footage she knows to be her apparently 'dead' ex-husband, who is running a diving school for tourists on the island of Santa Alicia, evidently under an alias.

That is shocking enough, but then it becomes apparent that the young man working next to her ex-husband in the video footage is the long lost son of the film's title. Chace has to wait until nearly twenty minutes into the film to make his appearance in this holiday video footage and even then it is only for a few seconds; appropriately perhaps given his latterday sex symbol status, he does so with his shirt off and wearing only a pair of shorts, preparing the tourist boat for a four-day cruise. As he chats to the hand-held video camera, Kristen realises that he is in fact her son; she rewinds the tape and freezes the picture on her ex-husband. That's when it dawns on her – they are both still alive. Kristen later discovers that the 'fatal' boat accident was in fact faked and that both her husband and 18-year-old son are alive and living on a Caribbean island. The entire ruse was in order for the husband to gain full custody of the son.

She discovers the exact location of the two men and learns from locals that her son is very popular. 'He's shaping up to be a real heartbreaker with the holiday girls that come in during the season,' one local tells her, which all Chace fans would certainly agree with! She eventually tracks down their boat and Chace reappears, this time in even fewer clothes, snorkelling around the harbour.

The handsome young man chats with Kristen and makes her feel very welcome, oblivious to their true relationship. He tells her he is Canadian and to her shock recounts how his mother died in a fire when he was only three years old. He later waxes lyrical about the travels he has been on with his father and proudly tells how his dad makes businesses and sells them on before relocating again.

From a technical point of view, Chace's dialogue seems very natural and fluid and does not fall victim to the stunted and wooden acting that so many made-for-TV films suffer from. From hereon in, it is he and Gabrielle who are the stars of the movie and the obvious highlights of the film. When Chace's character tells Kristen about his 'dead' mother, there is a genuine sense of dramatic tension that belies the humble made-for-TV backdrop.

Kristen admires her son from a distance – although for different reasons to most of the audience! – and when her ex-husband is caught trying to abscond again, he admits to Chace about who she actually is. Once mother and son are reunited, the realisation of what has happened leads to many troubling questions. Sadly, in gaining a mother, Chace's character loses his father, as his dad sails off into a storm and is later marooned on a desert island. Meanwhile, Chace's character and his mum head back to LA to start a new life.

It's a sign of Chace's latterday fame that despite the heart-wrenching plot and the emotionally laden storyline, most of the comments online about the movie centre around his looks, perhaps the favourite being, 'OMG, Chace is a hawtiee!' Although Chace's character didn't have the majority of dialogue, with the focus mostly on Gabrielle, he made sufficient impact to turn heads both for his looks and acting abilities.

Speaking to Christopher Bollen of *Interview Magazine*, however, Chace was rather awkward when asked about this early foray into acting. 'At that point I'm obviously taking anything I could get. I'm thinking, *Oh god. How do I even, like, craft this into something believable?* The woman they cast as my mom was like, 36 and smoking hot. She still is!' Chace became good friends with Gabrielle Anwar on set and has remained so ever since.

Her beauty and youthful looks caused Chace to worry about the credibility of his character's authenticity, namely with such a 'hot' mother being so young: 'This is going to look like I'm attracted to her – like when she finds me, I'm not supposed to know she's my mom, you know?' There were other equally obvious question marks surrounding the movie: when the 'reveal' exposes Chace as the long lost son of the film's title, the ex-husband and wife get on with surprisingly civility after a philosophical 'He's a good kid' platitude from a mother who has spent 14 years of torture grieving for a boy she has now discovered is alive. After his father heads off into the darkened stormy skies, Chace's character is next seen chatting merrily with his 'new' mother, heading off to LA seemingly without a care in the world, with no apparent sense of confusion, anger or bewilderment. It feels like an emotional loose end.

Critics are usually very snooty about so-called 'made-for-TV' films such as this; often the plots are derided, formulaic and very weak and the cast are usually mostly first-timers or those struggling for success. The satirical cartoon series *Family Guy* once spoofed the channel as 'Television for Idiots', including the movie *Men are Terrible and Will Hurt You Because This Is Lifetime*.

However, the flipside of this rather negative view is that such projects are also a priceless proving ground for many actors and there is a very long list of massive film and TV stars who have started off in this genre. Likewise, the directors behind such projects are often harshly scoffed for similar reasons; yet Brian Trenchard-Smith who headed up *Long Lost Son* is in fact cited by none other than Quentin Tarantino as one of the *Pulp Fiction* mastermind's favourite directors. The quirky sense of humour and large scale of Trenchard-Smith's work even led to an award-winning documentary about his early career called *Not Quite Hollywood*. The director also had a knack for discovering new talent, having premiered a 15-year-old Nicole Kidman in 1983's *BMX Bandits*. Similarly, when he worked with Chace, it was obvious to the director that here was a new star with great potential: 'I knew from his first scene, he was going to be hot,' Trenchard-Smith would later say.

Critics seemed to agree; Gabrielle Anwar was widely praised for her part but so Chace was too. Take this quote from Andrew L Urban on UrbanCineFile.com: 'It's Gabrielle Anwar's performance … that makes the film so engaging [and] her 18-year-old son [is] played effortlessly by the handsome and likeable Chace Crawford.' Other reviews were less flattering about the film but indirectly hailed Chace, such as this quote from the rather fantastic and funny www.mothermayisleepwithlifetime.blogspot.com: 'If you insist on watching this movie, fast forward to about the middle, once a hot teenage kid with his shirt off appears.'

It is simply not true that Chace's screen debut made him an overnight star; in fact, most fans were not even aware of this opening performance until long after he had made it big in *Gossip Girl*. However, what *Long Lost Son* did achieve was a solid start for Chace's acting career – as one of the stand-out actors in the film, he had made his first mark.

CHAPTER 3

Warlocks and Worries

'There have been a few girls that have gotten away that I wish I could put a spell on – make them fall in love with me.'

Chace Crawford speaking at the time of his first cinematic movie release, words he would probably never have to use again.

ALTHOUGH *LONG LOST SON* was his first actual aired screen appearance, that made-for-TV movie wasn't actually the first professional acting work he'd experienced. In 2004, while still at Pepperdine, he had begun filming a supernatural thriller called *Covenant*. This was a film intended for cinematic release, and as such Chace's first mainstream movie role. Filming began in Canada in 2004 but the actual movie's release was not until December 2006 by which time *Long Lost Son* had earned the right to be called Chace's first on-screen outing.

How Chace came to win the role in this new movie is typical of his ambition: he had sent a videotape of himself to the producers and received a request to be met in person, a 'call back'. That call back had led to auditions and Chace was exhilarated to win the role of Tyler, a 16-year-old warlock.

Directed by Renny Harlin, who was at the helm of *Cliffhanger*, as well as movies from the *Die Hard* franchise, and written by J S Cardone, *Covenant* recounts the tale of five seventeenth-century families from the Ipswich Colony of Massachusetts, who were supernaturally possessed with 'The Power' and formed a vow of silence in order to avoid being killed by the witch-hunting gangs that were prowling the new territory in those dark years. However, one family was a rogue spirit and was banished from the Covenant, mysteriously disappearing without a trace for centuries, only to turn up in modern-day America. (It is a common misconception that *Covenant* was based around a cartoon or graphic novel but this is not the case. There is a comic book of the same name, but this is unrelated to Chace's movie debut. Matters were made more complicated by the fact that a graphic novel of the movie was also later made.)

Descendants of these original five families have since settled in the town of Spencer and it is their intertwining lives that the film is focused around. As teenage warlocks, the sons of that seventeenth-century coven of witches have all been born with supernatural powers such as invincibility, shape-shifting, flight and super-strength. But each time the four 'Sons of Ipswich' use some of their addictive powers, they age prematurely, disastrously eroding their own life expectancy ... and they soon start to be hunted and haunted by so-called 'darklings', undead visions bent on destroying them.

These four teenage men are the central characters of the film; Chace plays Tyler Simms, the youngest of the foursome, and it is a sign of his still fledgling career that in the opening credits his name is only the sixth to flash up on-screen. Talking about his character in a promo interview for the film, Chace described him thus: '[Tyler's] kind of the youngest one. He's a junior in high school and he looks up to the other boys. He's kinda the rookie guy that just wants to use the power and be along for the joyride. It's a fun character, just kind of happy go lucky.'

The movie begins when a student is found dead of an apparent 'overdose' following an illicit beach party; thereafter dark secrets begin to unfold. It is the return of the 'long lost' fifth family's son that ramps up the horror. Confusingly, the 'long lost son' this time is also called Chace, albeit his character rather than the actor! This child was orphaned of his adoptive parents in a car accident aged only two, and it is revealed that this kid is the malevolent and vengeful fifth 'son' returning to wreak havoc on the other four warlocks. A climactic battle ensues between the lead Caleb and the evil

Chace, with our Mr Crawford nowhere to be seen. Good conquers evil ... but as with many horror movie endings, evil might come back. If a sequel gets commissioned.

The Sony Screen Gems film is a very much more polished and bigger budget affair than *Long Lost Son*. As *People* magazine put it, the film is 'one of those scary movies with pretty people'. As well as the notable young cast, there is a credible soundtrack which includes the likes of White Zombie and Killing Joke.

Chace himself modestly called his contribution merely 'a peripheral role'. It's true that his character is probably the most understated of the four 'Sons'; Steven Strait takes the lead role as Caleb opposite Laura Ramsey playing Sarah. And there are lengthy sections of the film when Chace makes no appearance whatsoever. His six-pack makes a showing in the swimming pool and shower scene while a subsequent swimming race ups the 'hunk' quota with rather obvious lashings of torso. When Chace does appear, he looks strikingly young, easily accommodating his character's sixteen years. In a jovial nod to his character's deference to others, when asked what his favourite scene was, he said, 'There's a group scene where we're all at Nicky's Bar [but] ... any close-up on me, that's my favourite!'

The film utilises many of the horror clichés, such as dark, spooky buildings, thunderstorms, cavernous crypts filled with candles (surely it must takes ages to light them all?), mysterious figures hiding in shadows and an ending that blatantly leaves open the opportunity for a sequel when the key 'bad guy' is nowhere to be found. In fact, some observers might suggest there were more stereotypes on offer here than in Chace's more 'unfashionable' made-for-TV debut film.

The plot is fairly slow-moving as indeed is the dialogue at times, and although the sense of suspense does ramp up as the film's climax approaches, there were some critics who felt the film was padded out, overweight and dwelled too obviously on the four male hunks in the lead roles. Not that any Chace Crawford fans were complaining about that! When Chace does have dialogue, it's fair to say there's a certain intensity that later fans of *Gossip Girl* would recognise.

It was quite a physical film for Chace too, with the four lead males often being thrown through the air, flying over the heads of other cast members or being smashed into walls and windows in violent fights. Chace's already toned physique was put through the mill as there were at least two swimming sessions per day to meet the target of twelve hours a week training in the pool that the producers desired – mindful of the inevitable emphasis on the boys' looks but also so that the crucial 'swimming pool' scene in the movie looked legitimate.

Further, before filming began Chace was required to train for weeks on so-called 'wire work', where an actor is strapped to a heavyweight safety wire, which will later be used for filming a 'flying' sequence. To make any such flying action look realistic takes a great deal of skill and also considerable physical prowess, but Chace relished the challenge: 'We did a lot of wire work and spent a lot of time at the gym. That was probably one of the most fun aspects of the whole shoot actually – getting to go and practise on this really cool wire rigging computerised motion kind of set. It was really fun to get on there and go to town on it – it was just great.' Cheekily, he added, 'There were no real-life warlocks though. It was definitely all stunts and what not!' He has also said that he likes to do 'all his own stunts' wherever possible as he feels this make the footage look more authentic and 'real'.

One example of his eagerness to inject all his scenes with authenticity actually came with the very first shot of the movie. The four teenage warlocks are shown walking to a cliff's edge, looking down at a beach party under way. Then, without warning, they simply walk off the edge, but instead of plummeting to their deaths, they gently float to the sandy ground below. Like much of the film, this effect was created against a green screen and this was Chace's first experience of this technology, which inevitably makes new demands on any actor: 'We were just stood still in the middle of a studio with some green screen around us at 9 a.m. So we had to deal with that – being completely stationary and acting like we're falling off the edge of a cliff.' Chace's fall was particularly difficult as his character dropped off backwards! Funnily, the one 'stunt' he says he would not undertake is any scene with spiders which in real life he doesn't like at all!

The supernatural backdrop to the film meant that many of the sequences were shot at night and in fact the whole of the first month was filmed during night-time, with five days on and Monday/Tuesday off. These night shifts were particularly tiring and in their downtime most of the cast just slept. Another challenge was the bitterly cold weather in Canada, which for Chace – a resident of Malibu – came as quite a shock! At one point when filming near a lake, the water had completely frozen solid. He got in the habit of taking very hot showers between takes just to stay warm. Asked if the cast found other ways to 'keep warm', Chace's fellow cast member Toby replied with a wry smile: 'We don't drink! What is sex? No, we got along really well, guys and girls, from day one. There are no assholes around. We've been out around Montreal, it's a great town!'

As it was Chace's first experience of a cinematic movie, he was understandably curious to see how the director Renny operated, but he was quickly put at ease; indeed, the director and cast got along famously and would even socialise in the (very few!) days off from shooting. Chace is on record as saying that Renny's style was to let the actors enjoy some creative expression with their characters in order to get the best out of them and Crawford really enjoyed this liberal approach.

It wasn't just the director that Chace had to impress though – none other than the president and vice-president of Sony Entertainment were frequently on set, adding to the pressure on the young actor. Both executives were very proactive in their opinions and would take the cast out for dinner on more than one occasion to discuss certain scenes but also just to relax. Chace wasn't the only inexperienced actor on set – with the exception of Steve Strait, most of the cast were relative newcomers.

Any fears that *Covenant* might be a commercial flop were dismissed brilliantly when it debuted at Number 1 in the film charts, taking $9 million in its first weekend, eventually grossing more than $23 million. That said, the box office success was in stark comparison to the media reception – the movie was widely panned, with critics arguing it was a poor man's *Lost Boys* (a cult classic horror movie from the 1980s that had openly been cited as an influence by the film company and was also a movie that Chace himself said was one of his all-time favourites) and an inferior relative of many horror films and action movies such as *Matrix*. Equally negative comparisons were made to the huge smash show *Buffy The Vampire Slayer*. The influential Rotten Tomatoes website even placed it at Number 31 in its list of the decade's 'Worst of the Worst'. Other media sources pointed to the fact it had been a quiet weekend for new movies and thus hitting Number 1 was somehow less of an achievement.

The critics' pens were sharpened with such quotes as this from *Time Out*: 'Flying scenes, frat-boy face-offs and pyrotechnic punch-ups are punctuated by excruciating expository dialogue, while a nasty whiff of homophobia sits uneasily with the many lingering shots of naked male torsos.' The *Boston Phoenix* said simply it was 'an unbewitching brew of clichés,' while the *Daily Mirror* said, '*Covenant* looks less like a movie and more like an extended boy-band video – and with about the same amount of depth.'

It was comments such as this last remark that threatened to damage Chace's fledgling career most seriously. With striking looks such as his, it is all too easy to be stereotyped into 'hunk' roles and struggle forever after to be taken seriously. 'Himbo' is the unkind phrase that settles on such actors. It was his first taste of the movies, and also his first taste of a critic's panning. The question was: did Chace have what it took to break out of this mould?

In a style that would soon become typical of his positive attitude, Chace could only see benefits from having acted in *Covenant*. Speaking with *Female First* magazine, he made no secret of the fact he felt he was lucky to have landed the role: 'Actually it has taken some getting used to. It was a very surreal experience for me to be honest. It was crazy because it was like my first real job, so to be in a big studio feature film I'm very fortunate in a big way.' He had also received a considerable amount of fan mail and was keen to show his gratitude: 'The people who liked [*Covenant*] really liked it – it's good to have those fans.'

An interesting by-product of filming *Covenant* was that it gave Chace a taste for studying again, albeit acting rather than the journalism he had started to major in back at Pepperdine. Some of the cast of the film had academic backgrounds in acting, such as Toby Hemingway who had a BA in theatre, and Chace respected and was drawn to this more technical approach. Chace also went to see co-star Sebastian Strait during a role on Broadway and this gave the future *Gossip Girl* actor a taste for acting on the stage that he retains to this day.

It was after the release of *Covenant* that Chase was asked to sign his first autograph. He has since admitted that this was a strange feeling – his modesty told him it was 'surreal' and even 'useless' but at the same time he was delighted and not about to take this newfound celebrity for granted. Even his dad phoned and asked him if he could send some signed photos to give out to a few friends!

CHAPTER 4

Gossip Girl

'[I'm also working on] *Gossip Girl* – a pilot of a TV show that I just shot in New York last month. It's based on a book series – a very popular series, mainly with the girls here in America. It's based on this group of teenagers from an elite private school in New York. They're the popular kids in Manhattan … It's got a good chance of being picked up and a good shot of being a real hit series in the fall, so keep an eye out … '

Chace Crawford speaking to *Female First* magazine in early 2007, before the launch of *Gossip Girl*.

2007 WAS THE YEAR that Chace Crawford exploded on to the scene. He began the year as an aspiring young actor with a low-key made-for-TV movie on his CV as well as a Number 1 film that had been critically panned. He would end

2007 as one of the hottest new actors on the planet ... how did this happen? Two words: *Gossip Girl*.

The major US TV networks receive hundreds of pitches for new shows each season. Once the elimination process has whittled the numbers down, about 20 will be roughly made into a pilot to test audience interest; roughly a quarter will actually turn into TV shows. In this tough business not all of these survive beyond the first season.

When it was announced that the same team behind *The* OC (the hit teen drama set in Orange Country, California) were creating a new show, there was always going to be huge interest from actors and their agents. Chace was given the script for the pilot of *Gossip Girl* in January 2007 by his new agent; he was very aware of Josh Schwartz's reputation because of *The* OC and so although at first look he felt it was 'typical teen stuff', he also knew it would be very high quality. Chace admits that he wasn't a huge fan of that show; he liked it and watched it, but he wasn't an obsessive. 'I did watch *The* OC a little bit, though,' he told Josh Clinton. 'Back when I was a freshman in college, that was the show to watch. We had our Wednesday night viewing parties and stuff. There was always some great melodrama going on in that show.' The scale of the success of the new TV show would soon take him by surprise: 'Little did I know how insanely popular this series of books were with younger gals ... '

Chace was referring to the fact that the new show was based on the bestselling novels by Cecily von Ziegesar, which have sold millions of copies around the world. The books centred around the lives and love interests of a group of girls from Constance Billboard School for Girls, a private elite school in New York's Upper East Side. Originally published in 2002, the books ran to eleven novels, with a prequel and the sequel issued too, proof positive that there was a rich vein of material for any TV show to mine. As with the forthcoming TV series, the content of the novels – at times explicit and often risky – was criticised heavily in some quarters for being inappropriate for a teenage readership. American writer Naomi Wolf called the books 'corruption with a cute overlay'. Notably, the eventual TV series would have some substantial differences to the book series, but these changes made no difference to either project's runaway success.

Back at the auditions for the TV show of the same name, if Chace thought he was a shoe-in, he was in for a shock. Shows like *The OC* don't just get made off the cuff, and Schwartz and his crew are very well known for being absolutely meticulous in their preparation and groundwork. And so the casting process for *Gossip Girl* would prove to be no exception: Chace himself was a hit with the producers from day one in auditions but even so, he was called back six times. Some of these auditions are online and Chace looks extremely young; his acting is adept, despite being in an empty audition room, and on occasion he has to act back to staffers from the production team rather than fellow actors.

Chace had only been acting seriously for three years so as yet he didn't have a formal showreel; he also felt 'pretty new to all of this … it was a learning process'. Nonetheless, he took to the auditions like a natural and kept being called back. His energy was kept high by the appeal of the character he was auditioning for, a rich kid called Nate Archibald: '[On] the first read I thought Nate was totally attainable for me and something I was interested in,' he told Josh Clinton of *Prime Time Pulse*. 'I went in prepared and met with Josh and Stephanie, the director, and casting director, and I guess they liked me. I went in again and again to audition.'

Perhaps not surprisingly given the show's creative team, competition for the lead roles was intense. Although Chace had a couple of movies under his belt, he was relatively inexperienced compared to many of the handsome actors walking in to auditions. Yet his agent was convinced that Chace was the man for the job: 'I think I hit six [auditions],' he told thestar.com, 'The producers were always nice to me and kept calling me back. So I knew I had a chance.'

On his final reading, Chace was paired up with fellow Texan native Leighton Meester who had already been officially cast as Blair Waldorf. 'Leighton was fantastic when I got to read with her,' he later told *MediaBlvd*. 'When I met her and the rest of the cast, I knew it could be something good.'

The final decision over who would get the part of Nate Archibald was left to former actor-turned-CBS president Les

Moonves and Chace got the call to star in the pilot! This did not mean that he was home and dry however. Many pilots are made each year and only a few get to be commissioned and launched as a series – as little as 25 per cent. Pilots often have different actors or actresses in them compared to the final series, so even getting this far was no guarantee of Chace's success. Even if he secured the role of Nate, there was also no guarantee as very often entire characters get written out. Chace's career was still on a knife-edge.

His inexperience was something which he knew stacked the odds again him yet at the same time he seemed to rise to this challenge. Speaking to *MediaBlvd* magazine, he said, 'I've felt like an outsider for the last three years in this business. All the names get the jobs. It's such a political thing. When it gets down to the finals, there's five guys and the producers lay out the resumés. I was always fighting that. I think you have to get over that and start the snowball towards you.'

Despite his admitted relative inexperience, Chace was fully aware of the precarious nature of pilots and the TV commissioning process. He'd already worked two previous pilot seasons, but was undeterred – those who have worked with him all comment on the burning ambition and desire to act that is at the core of his personality. So, when it came to his third so-called 'pilot season', he worked incredibly hard to impress as many executives as possible. As well as the *Gossip Girl* pilot, he also got 'test deal' for a show called *Gravity* – also on CW – which never materialised and a show for MBC too, called *Zip*. So conversely, *Gossip Girl* was by no means assured of capturing Chace's services. With this in mind, Chace sat down with Josh Schwartz and discussed the process and how he was being received; he was told that he was very much one of the front-runners and so along with his agent he decided to focus on *Gossip Girl*. 'It was a good gamble!' he later noted.

His character is Nate Archibald, a stunningly handsome and amenable kid from a very wealthy family who was so alluring that he would sleep with the show's two lead females in the very first episode! As with the source material, Nate was the central character, perhaps even more so in the novels. In the novels he is a lacrosse player at the prestigious St Jude's School for Boys, the son of a French socialite and a wealthy banker. In the TV show his father is described as a wealthy businessman but he does attend the same private school.

Viewers often class the pilot of a series as the 'first' episode and avid fans pride themselves on knowing all about the pilot and how it differs from the eventual series run. Chace was clever with his own personal videotape of the pilot – he showed it to a number of 'real' *Gossip Girl* kids, young adults who actually live the life that the show mimics. He let them watch the pilot and then asked if it was remotely authentic and the answer was a very positive yes!

The link to shows like *The OC* was clear. The complicated love lives of the rich elite in California's Orange County was mirrored in *Gossip Girl* by the equally complex relationships of ultra-wealthy socialites in Upper Manhattan. The platinum credit cards with unlimited spending ceilings, exclusive restaurants and colossal apartments really are the life of this social elite. To give this some context, to buy a one-bed apartment in one of Upper Manhattan's more prestigious blocks would set you back at least $1.5 million; you want to buy a large five-bedroom penthouse? Best set aside at least $10 million. A big townhouse? Think $30–40 million. Each square foot – that's twelve inches by twelve inches of carpet – will cost you at least $1,500 minimum.

The Upper East Side of Manhattan is situated between Central Park and the East River, bordered by 59th Street and 96th Street, as well as the river and Fifth Avenue on Central Park. It is the single most prestigious area to live in the Big Apple, not least by virtue of the cost of homes, and is one of the most exclusive city neighbourhoods in the entire world. The Upper East Side is reputed to contain the greatest concentration of wealth on earth.

This being the case, it attracts very successful people from all walks of life and these are sometimes the sort of folk who will win at all costs. The ability to have anything in life at a price can also sometimes – though not always of course – erode a person's sense of reality and it is this rarefied atmosphere of ultra-wealth that we see has corrupted quite a few of the faces and characters who appear in *Gossip Girl*.

This dynamic has of course been used by Hollywood many times before: among the films which feature the Upper East Side are classics such as *Breakfast At Tiffany's*, *Live and Let Die*, *The Bonfire of the Vanities*, *Eyes Wide Shut* and *American Psycho*. TV is often drawn to the exclusive zip codes of this area too, with shows such as *Friends*, *Diff'rent Strokes*, *Sex and the City* and *Ugly Betty* all being filmed there. Inevitably the area attracts many famous and highly successful residents in real life too, with notable residents including Lady Ga Ga, Sarah Michelle Gellar and Madonna, who paid $40 million for her house there in 2009.

This is the lavish surrounding for *Gossip Girl*'s pilot episode. Opening with 'It Girl' Serena on a train into Manhattan, the pilot episode sees Serena return to the glamorous Upper East Side social circles that *Gossip Girl* chronicles. It isn't long before we are at a glitzy NY party with waiters, rich guests and pearls the size of tennis balls. The narrator of the show is the anonymous blogger Gossip Girl who sends texts and blogs about the friendships and relationships within a group of New York socialites, including Serena van der Woodsen (Blake Lively) and Blair Waldorf (Leighton Meester) as the two centres of attention, then also the boys and girls in their circles such as Dan (Penn Badgley), Nate (Chace), Jenny (Taylor Momsen), Chuck (Ed Westwick), Vanessa (Jessica Szohr), Lily (Kelly Rutherford) and Rufus (Matthew Settle).

Chace's first appearance on-screen is at this party, dressed in a smart suit and blue tie, talking to his overbearing father and his friends about his next educational step (his fashion sense in the pilot is sophisticated, mainly formal suits and less-than-casual wear). Immediately it is obvious that there is a tension between what Nate wants and what his father thinks is best. Then his girlfriend Blair Waldorf pounces on him just as the infamous Serena turns up at the party; Nate is clearly keen to see Serena again and we immediately realise that Nate may have had a 'thing' for the blond Serena in the past. When Blair crosses the room to meet her supposed 'BFF' Serena, it's all vacuous, insincere air kisses and meaningless chit-chat. Nate's first love triangle is underway and the pilot is only a few minutes old!

The role of the Gossip Girl is pivotal to the entire show and we see that everyone is logging on to her website to keep up with the latest gossip, personal snippets, photos, rumours and so on. As with the show itself, most of the characters on-screen seem to want to deny they look at the site, but actually they love it! In fact, the abbreviations of the website referring to 'S' and 'B' etc. are used by most of the characters in real life too, confirming that they are all living out and/or catching up with the *Gossip Girl* blog.

The next scene in the pilot sees Nate and his long-time childhood friend Chuck Bass on a bus talking about a girl. Chuck – played by Ed Westwick of course! – is the dark foil to Nate's more honest personality. The way that Chuck describes 'violating' this one particular girl's innocence immediately appalls his friend Nate, setting out early on the very different moral values of the two pals. Nate, it seems, is clearly the All-American good guy; Chuck obviously isn't! Chace is brilliantly cast, as from a purely physical point of view he ticks every box in the stereotypical US definition of a hunk. The dynamic between Nate and Chuck underpins much of *Gossip Girl*, something we see very early on in the pilot: the contrasting moral values, the different styles, the totally different approach to women and so on. Despite all these differences, Nate and Chuck are very much a case of 'opposites attract'; their friendship is a deep and strangely reliant one.

With Blair trying to seduce Nate, he is now in a dilemma, with thoughts of the recently returned Serena in his mind. We soon discover that Nate and Serena had kissed at a wedding the previous year and that was why she had to leave town. The raunchy wedding scene of S and N kissing also sets the tone for the more explicit nature of the show, which would go on to cause much controversy and negative headlines. The revelation of the wedding kiss leads to Nate and Blair breaking up, which is not a popular move with his father, who is trying to negotiate a business deal with Blair's mother.

Nate is suppressed, suffocated, his father's money-making and power struggles obviously taking precedence over his needs. The viewer quickly feels sympathy for Nate, which only makes him even more endearing and attractive (Blair has an overbearing parent too!). He is immersed in but apparently not entirely comfortable with all the luxurious superficialities of life on the Upper East Side, and this theme is a recurring one that we see Nate struggle with – later in the first season he gets sucked into a gambling scam after being drawn towards a wealthy old school pal who appears to enjoy a more liberal life of travelling the world and being free of society's expectations.

Yet when Nate reassures Blair that he won't talk to Serena or even consider she exists any more, we all know this isn't going to happen! So Nate is lying, although at the time he says those words, he (kind of) believes them. The words will, of course, turn out to be completely hollow.

The pilot is very much focused on Nate/Chace and his relationship with Blair, Serena, his father and his sense of frustration at not being able to live his life as he wants. When Serena turns up at another party uninvited, it all kicks off, with Blair and Nate arguing again, everyone in the room checking their phones for text updates and Chuck hovering like a black widow spider over a young girl called Jenny. At the end of the pilot, a yellow cab drives off into the Manhattan night with Serena, Jenny and her brother Dan all safely inside, while Nate and Chuck watch, both with completely different agendas! It's a thrilling, compelling and addictive episode.

Chace was sure the pilot would lead to a full series: 'I was really impressed with the look and the music,' he told *MediaBlvd*. 'It was unbelievable. There's no weak links on anything, from the acting to the directing to the lighting. It all came together very nicely.' At the same time, looking back,

Chace thinks that the pilot was perhaps a little too raunchy, as he told www.thestar.com: 'They added a scene with my father to show where Nate is coming from. It's really not about sex as much as having too much of everything.'

The pilot also set a great precedent for the show's evocative soundtrack. Over the four seasons to date, there have been some great songs used to ramp up the atmosphere, with contributions from Rihanna, the late, great Amy Winehouse, Albert Hammond Jr. and Angels and Airwaves.

When the news came through that CW had decided to fund the entire series, it was a massive moment for Chace as well as all the other cast members. One practicality was that Chace had to relocate to New York for filming. He was thrilled to be in the Big Apple. Previously he'd only visited as a Texan tourist when he was just 16 and even then had only done all the obvious sight-seeing tours that you do on holiday. This time around, city life was a great new experience for Chace: 'I completely fell in love with New York when we were filming the pilot.' After filming he would party, eat at cool restaurants and shoot pool in cool bars with his friends, so it's perhaps not hard to see why the city holds such a big attraction for him! He loves the fact that you can get food 24/7, he enjoys the city's famous street corner hot dog stands and when he was chatting to one interviewer about being fairly rudimentary at cooking, co-star Ed Westwick butted in and pointed out he was missing a trick: 'It's about knowing how to pick up the phone and order something!'

Even before the first episode of *Gossip Girl* aired, the hype surrounding the show and the stellar reputation of the writers and producers suggested that it was about to be a massive smash hit. Chace was acutely aware of this yet was disarmingly honest about the effects and repercussions this might have on his life, as he told *MediaBlvd*: 'I'm not prepared at all, to be honest. I'm taking it day by day. It's insane. I want to take it episode by episode and just make sure my work is good. The rest, I hope, will take care of itself.'

Chace fans didn't have to wait long for the first glimpse of their man. Nate/Chace appears nearly seven minutes into the first episode, woken by a phone call from Blair to remind him of the brunch event. It turns out he is in the same room as Chuck who has been kept company by two women, while Nate has slept alone on the couch! They chat about the night before and it's clear that the two mates are somehow a perfect foil for each other. Chace heads off to the brunch in full dinner jacket attire, bumping into Serena's mother and doing a very bad job of trying to be indifferent about her daughter. The N S B love triangle takes on a new angle when Serena's new date, Dan, and Nate realise that they are both chasing her affections. At the climactic brunch later, Serena and Nate secretly meet up – with Nate again wearing a designer suit – but Blair invites herself too and there is yet another argumentative confrontation. As the opening episode closes, it is revealed that Serena slept with Nate at last year's wedding after all, and a fight ensues when Chuck calls Dan's sister a slut. Nate exits the episode with his relationship with Blair nearly in ruins, lying next to her in bed attempting to reconciliate. Not for the first time, we witness Blair and Nate's on-off relationship spiral out of control. With Blair holding Chace/Nate's hand as the end music starts to roll, the first episode of *Gossip Girl* leaves a lot of questions unanswered. Serena ends the episode by binning her mobile, but it clearly won't prove to be so easy to lose her connections with the Upper East Side elite.

Chace was quite literally an unknown before that debut episode aired. Yet by then, anticipation for the new show had reached sufficient heights that his celebrity was almost running away from the reality. Writing for thestar.com, Jim Bawden said: 'These are Chace Crawford's last, precious days of anonymity. There will now be a moment's silence for you to ask: "Who the heck is Chace Crawford?" Tune in tonight on the CW and you won't have to ask again.'

Chace himself seemed equally unaware of what was about to happen – namely that his life would never be the same again. In one sense, this was never inevitable as each year many new TV series are piloted and debuted and most fall by the wayside; however, there was an endearing naïveté to his apparently blissful innocence: 'I really don't know what to expect.' He also admitted to last-minute nerves: '[It's] nerve-racking,' he told thestar.com. 'It puts on a lot of pressure. You have to prepare for either outcome. Whether it's a flop from the hype or it lives up to the hype. I'm completely confident in it though.'

Gossip Girl was quickly being tagged as 'The OC Goes East' but what started off initially as a flattering comparison would soon turn into an outdated parallel, as *Gossip Girl* became an instant ratings smash. Reviews were brilliant with many focusing on Chace's performance; the following day, the opening episode of *Gossip Girl* was being talked about all over America. One thing was immediately clear: the CW network had a major hit on their hands.

However, with an entire season to shoot, no one had time to rest on their laurels and toast the huge success of the opening episode. Filming often spilled out on to the streets of the world's biggest film set, Manhattan. Initially there had been talk of filming in Vancouver or even possibly Los Angeles, but with the Big Apple taking such a prominent role in the show, the producers decided to plump for the real deal. They used the same stages as had been utilised by the award-winning *Sopranos* and as such the show has a very authentic feel.

With many of the young cast being unknowns, these early days of filming were a simple pleasure. Chace was unashamed about his relative inexperience: 'It's all new to me. The younger actors are sticking together – it's the only way to survive the craziness. Right now we can shoot in Central Park and nobody bothers us.' Not for long …

Working with the two famous TV geniuses Schwartz and Savage was a real pleasure for Chace, as he told Josh Clinton:

'Oh man, they're great. They were on every day for the pilot and were there for the first few episodes ... Josh was the youngest television creator ever at 26 when he created *The OC*. It's so cool. They have the lingo down, they have the cutting-edge writing that flows like butter. It's unbelievable. It's been great ... Stephanie is so great. You can always call her up and count on her help. They are always so conducive to what you want to do. We all hang out when they are in town, so it's like a big family.'

As the show's fame accelerated in those heady first few weeks of broadcast, quiet days out filming in Manhattan became a thing of the past. Pretty soon, the security around the shoots was manic: 'Yeah, it can be rather difficult,' Chace explained to *TV Interviews* magazine, 'but we're all used to it ... It can be annoying on location when photographers are in your line of vision, snapping away. They're like little wasps that fly around you! It's also funny with girls – sometimes, after 3.30 p.m. when school's gone out, if one of them sees you, the viral text messaging starts! Then after an hour you turn around and there's like 100 of them ... with their moms. It's pretty cool though.' He also noticed that it wasn't just the obvious teenage girl fans who were coming along to the filming either; over time, as the show's profile grew, he started to spot wealthy Upper East Side New Yorkers – namely the very same people the show was fictionalising – coming along to watch too.

To be fair, his own mum had also visited the city 'to see what all the fuss is about!' Endearingly, Chace took her to eat at Butter, a restaurant/bar that features in *Gossip Girl*, and later took her to some other local bars because she'd said she wanted him to 'show me one of those little *Gossip Girl* places!'

Chace loves walking around the city – although NY is crammed with traffic, Chace will stroll around and enjoys the fact he doesn't always need to drive. He's also on record saying he finds the diversity of the Big Apple very appealing and has learned a lot from being around so many different cultures compared to the more conservative lifestyle usually found in Texas. 'It's infectious, it's a change of pace for me.' He's also said, 'New York's a big playground. I have a bike, and I'm really into just being outside. Especially in the summertime. The winters could eventually get to me [though], I mean, I'm a southern boy, so I like that humidity!'

Intriguingly, although he was now well aware of the huge fan base surrounding the original books, he seemed reluctant to immerse himself too much in the paper version of *Gossip Girl*, as this quote from the *Boston Herald* suggests:

'I actually thought I owed it to the fans to read [the books]. I got halfway through the first one and realised we can do something else, take it where we want it to go. And I feel like the show is going to be able to stand on its own. We know the gist of our characters and know how it's supposed to be. I feel personally it kind of gets in my head if I read all twelve [books] or whatever there are.'

Actually Chace was not alone, with several of the key actors and actresses admitting that they hadn't read the series; most had in fact read some or all of the first book only. 'The books put a little bit of pressure on the expectations and all that jazz,' admitted Chace to *The CW Source*.

Back on the show, Nate's life is nothing if not a roller coaster. After the tumultuous introduction of the pilot and first episode, life doesn't get any easier for Chace's character. He seems incapable of making a final decision between Blair and Serena and it begins to feel like he wants whichever one he cannot have. Chace's fan base forgive him this indecision of course and from the writers' point of view, it allows *Gossip Girl* to repeatedly run the 'will they, won't they?' storyline that is so captivating to fans.

Nate/Chace's relationship with Chuck is also a complex one and as Season 1 progresses it becomes ever more complicated when Chuck sets his lecherous eyes on Blair. To be fair, Nate had messed Blair around a lot, so there could be no complaints, particularly as Nate had slept with Blair's own best friend Serena. The circles of love interest get ever more complicated and messy with each episode. Yet even after an affair with Blair, Chuck and Nate holiday in Monaco, for ever linked (although at this point Nate is oblivious to Chuck's deceit). Inevitably the secret gets out and a fight leaves Nate with neither his girlfriend nor his best friend. Again the show plugs sympathy for Nate before Season 1 ends with Chuck and Nate reconciled, that strange, intimate bond reaffirmed. Millions of Chace Crawford fans watched every episode obsessively and no doubt all were thinking how great it would be to offer him a shoulder to cry on!

So the first season of *Gossip Girl* was a huge smash hit. The Internet was buzzing with talk of the characters, the actors and actresses, the gossip, the clothes, every aspect of the show was being dissected and discussed. Only a few short months earlier Chace had been a relative unknown auditioning hopefully for the role of Nate Archibald. Yet by Christmas of 2007, he was one of the biggest new names in television. And there was far, far more to come ...

CHAPTER 5

Loaded With Fame

WITH CHACE'S TV PROFILE now so high due to the meteoric success of the first season of *Gossip Girl*, any film roles he undertook were bound to attract intense interest from the public and media alike. Next up on the big screen for him was *Loaded*, starring opposite Jesse Metcalfe in a film produced by Wingman Productions and directed by Alan Pao (*The Art of Travel*, *Strike*).

Jesse Metcalfe was a similarly feted and good-looking young actor who had found fame in the daytime drama *Passions* and then most notably on the ABC TV drama *Desperate Housewives*. His first movie role had been in *John Tucker Must Die*, so in a sense he was only slightly ahead of Chace in career terms. The cast also boasted soccer player turned actor Vinnie Jones, who had made his name playing for the famously brutal Wimbledon FC but after his retirement from football had successfully made a big name for himself in Hollywood with superb performances in films such as *Lock, Stock and Two Smoking Barrels* and *Gone in 60 Seconds*.

Loaded is set around the dark and sinister edges of the LA club scene. Metcalfe's character Tristan Price leads a privileged life and has a loving family but he becomes increasingly involved in a dangerous web of drugs and crime. Initially he is introduced as a 25-year-old wealthy UCLA student with a high-flying career in law ahead of him, but one night after his birthday party he heads into the city to a go-go club ... and from then on his life starts to unravel. First off he hooks up with an unsavoury girl at the club which leads him to be reacquainted with an old college friend (and now big-time drug dealer) Sebastian Cole (Corey Large). As the drug lord abuses his 'friendship' with Tristan to access the latter's wealthy family and friends, events spiral into a mess of guns, violence and increasingly desperate actions.

Chace appears as Hayden Price, the younger brother of Jesse Metcalfe's character. Again Chace's role was somewhat peripheral and his actual amount of screen time rather limited. In one scene when Chace and his character's girlfriend are smooching in a car, they are accosted by Johnny Messner's character and beaten up. The veteran actor played a neat trick on the pair of young stars by acting in character and genuinely intimidating them, so that the tension and fear on-screen became palpable. The scene is really quite uncomfortable and the violence and cruelty shown is disturbing – when his character Hayden is threatened by his neck being throttled, Chace seems genuinely short of breath and there is a real sadistic edge to the footage. Chace found it a strange experience but a brilliant learning curve: 'It was definitely one of the weirdest mixes of emotions I'd ever felt. I was really kinda pissed at him for a while. In the scene, it hurt! You can really imagine ... it really affected me.'

Regardless of his modest role, Chace clearly made a good impression on set. One of his co-stars, Monica Keena, was quoted as saying, 'I don't know how somebody that good-looking can still be so nice!' while Nathalie Kelley said he was going to be the next Brad Pitt!

The filming of the entire movie only took one month and that fast-paced momentum is definitely captured on the screen, as the energy and edge on set translates into the finished article. Chace and Jesse became good pals during the shoot and have remained friends since.

The film itself was a so-called 'straight to DVD' release, meaning it never had widespread cinematic distribution, generally regarded within Hollywood as the mark of an inferior project. Reviews for the movie are certainly rather mixed. On realmovienews.com, the writer said that,

'The filmmakers ask for a bit too much forgiveness of the viewer ... this creates a feeling of disbelief in both the driving plot and the other characters' insistence that they were not a part of Sebastian's larger plan. The script feels reminiscent of *The Hand That Rocks the Cradle*, *The Game*, and *Unlawful Entry*, and does not seem to add much originality to an already saturated genre.' In this review, like many others, Chace was not even mentioned. There were some positives however, such as this from *Sky Movies*: '[*Loaded*] goes off the rails to crowd-pleasing effect in a pacy ride that delivers its thrills with a glossy sheen.'

However, there was the overall sense that *Loaded* did not really take Chace's movie career forward. With *Gossip Girl* showing no signs of slowing down in ratings, there were clear indications that for now at least, Chace's small-screen profile was far bigger than his silver-screen persona.

Back at *Gossip Girl* Central, there were no such worries about mediocre reviews or limited commercial appeal. The show, even in its downtime, was creating a buzz on the Internet that was almost unprecedented. Fans of the show bought into the blogging focus of the narrator and there wasn't a day went by that a new site or blog influenced by the show was started. And more often than not, one character that everyone mentioned was Nate Archibald! As a consequence, Chace Crawford's fame quite literally exploded. In the aftermath of *Gossip Girl*'s first season, Chace realised that his life would never be the same again.

The most obvious reflection of the show's success was the huge number of fans who would turn up at any filming on the streets of Manhattan. While Chace was trying to work he would be bombarded with gifts and very often the screams of his fans would mean retakes. He constantly receives the more 'regular' fan worship presents – underwear, cuddly toys, food, pictures and letters – but he has also mentioned that one letter from a French fan that talked about how much the character of Nate meant to her was so touching that he kept it as a personal memento. Of course it works both ways and fans are desperate for items of his clothing, a clump of hair (!) or even on one occasion his half-drunk can of Coke. 'One day some girls formed a sort of doughnut shape, like a mob,' he told *Newsbeat*. 'We were trying to get to set and it was a bad time of day, 3.30 on a Friday when school was out. They all texted their friends and everyone came down. They were clawing at the clothes, they wanted [my] tie or Diet Coke can or anything. I had a lot of marriage proposals that day too, which was kind of funny.'

As the momentum behind *Gossip Girl* gathered pace, Chace noticed that it wasn't just young girls who wanted his attention, as this quote from *Vman* shows:

'I'll be out on the golf course, and some guy will come up to me, sort of sheepishly, and be like, "Hey, my wife really loves the show. Can I get a picture with you?" They're always super embarrassed. And I'm like, "C'mon man, you love the show." Women get their husbands or boyfriends sucked into it. I like to see that.' Chace himself also liked the idea of older fans, as he told *Extra*: '[The fan base] has changed a bit in that we have more fun with everyone … it's nice to hear it from the adults, the older crowd … '

A second aspect of the huge success of *Gossip Girl* and its impact on Chace's life is the massive volume of magazine, TV and radio interviews he has to do. At times, this can be exhausting but, along with Ed Westwick, Chace is one of the show's best promoters. Almost every interview asks him if he is single, who the hottest girl on set is and what's his dream date, his favourite look in a girl, his chat-up lines etc. He always seems to answer fairly diplomatically when it comes to 'Who is the best kisser on set?', choosing not to stoke the fires of any gossip about behind-the-scenes relationships. However, patient as he is, it must eventually get tiring to keep answering these sorts of questions.

It's noticeable that many interviewers meet him in the flesh and comment on his electric blue eyes (later, when he was filming a movie called *Twelve*, none other than 50 Cent was so impressed by the luminescence of his eyes that he called them 'Skyline eyes'). Mind you, other journalists comment as much about his 'trademark' bushy eyebrows! When he was a kid his mum used to occasionally tell him to pluck them but he says he doesn't like to be too preened and fake. Chace is clearly even more striking in person – in one interview with a British newspaper, the female journalist met Chace in a café and said that when he entered the room, there was an audible sigh of 'Aaaaahhhhh' from the women at various tables nearby.

Chace begins his
modelling career
very young!

Chace was a modest,
popular teenager at
school and a strong
sportsman who would
go on to be awarded
'Best Dressed' in his
senior year.

Classic Chace Crawford, those eyebrows, that hair!

The obvious friendship and camaraderie between Chace and Ed Westwick persuaded the pals to rent an apartment together for maximum *Gossip Boys* fun.

Having fun on set with *Gossip Girl* co-star Blake Lively, and her super-cute pup, Penny.

Good looks run in the family! Here is Chace with his grandmother and mum.

As Nate Archibald in *Gossip Girl*, Chace wears some of the finest designer suits and formalwear.

Opposite: Chace is very close to his sister, Candice. Here they are together at a party at the White House.

Chace pictured on set in 2011 with Liz Hurley, a photo which sent the GG blogs crazy!

Another reporter asked him the same question three times because when he answered, she was just sitting there, looking at him.

Due to the online nature of the show's success, a lot of promotion is on the web which Chace also enjoys. However, he tries to steer clear of the countless blogs – at the time of writing there are over 100 Facebook fan groups about the show – as he says these will sometimes be filled with 'hate'. Endearingly, he kept his Facebook and Myspace accounts open after his fame broke on *GG*, but soon realised that this was impossible to continue and eventually closed them all down. Since those innocent days he has recoiled completely from an online public presence: 'I'm the biggest believer in not talking,' he told Christopher Bollen. 'I don't Twitter or MySpace or Facebook. I want to keep to myself. I don't want to be out there. You have to keep some kind of control over who you are.' Given the intrusion into his private life that his fame has inevitably attracted, this instinct to be more insular is likely to just become even more important to him.

Chace's profile is such that he also has many YouTube and related clips online; indeed, several fans have compiled their own montages of Chace clips. There are even clips specifically about intimate aspects of his career and life, so for example you have one such snip called 'Private pictures of Chace and Ed'.

After the initial joyous naïveté of his early comments on fame had subsided, and it became clear that the sheer scale of his celebrity was starting to invade his privacy, he acknowledged that at times his success was having a negative impact on his 'normal' lifestyle.

Chace has to balance promoting the show and his films with what must be an ever-increasing invasion into his private life. So across the hundreds of interviews he does each year, we find out more and more of the minute detail about Chace's personal life: what his worst habit is (talking loudly on the phone), what skincare products he uses ('a good face wash by SkinCeuticals'), how he gets that famous hairstyle (Bumble and Bumble Styling Wax), and the fact he prefers dry shaving to wet. He wears Right Guard deodorant, prefers texting, boxers and stubble, but doesn't like nose-piercings on a girl or 'alien' sunglasses like the ones Paris Hilton wears. He likes fishing trips and mountain biking with friends, blondes *and* brunettes, and booty shorts worn with high socks. He's good at Wii tennis, but also loves Trivial Pursuit and Scrabble, he's good at grilling chicken and prefers loafers to cowboy boots.

It wasn't just what we knew about his tastes and preferences either, living a normal life day-to-day was becoming increasingly difficult. With paparazzi following his every move, someone even posted his home address on the Internet. Speaking to *ES* magazine, he said:

'I don't want to sound like I'm bitching, but it's gotten more difficult to connect with people on that innocent, level playing field … The process of meeting people has gotten pretty abstract. It could be a bit of paranoia thrown in there on my side, just being wary of other people's intentions, or people having preconceived notions of who I am.'

Reflecting on his rapid success, Chace has said that he thinks his 'cynical attitude' helped, in that he carried with him a realistic philosophy on his chances of success. He was naturally quite wary of the 'celebrity' folk. The super-celebrity that Chace experienced was 'overnight' in many ways, but that was also the case for much of the cast. He feels that his co-stars have coped well with the surge of fame and media attention. It's hard to overestimate just how big *Gossip Girl* became and how fast!

When *New York* magazine ran a cover feature on *Gossip Girl*, the tag line was 'Best Show Ever'. In another notable interview the strapline gave a fair indication of how Chace had gone from new face to new star in a matter of months, as it hailed, 'The hottest new property in Hollywood right now'. It helped that he was openly single, keeping the hopes and dreams of his ever-growing legion of fans alive. However, he was clearly slightly wary of the whole 'hunk' tag: 'It's weird you know, I still don't know what a heart-throb is. No one's yet managed to tell me exactly what that is. But it's really cool – I mean, I can't say that I don't like some of the attention but I just want to focus on my career now and I haven't really bought into the whole Hollywood scene.' By now Chace was considered among the most desirable actors on the planet.

Perhaps unusually for such a famous face, as his fame escalated he has found himself being drawn back to his roots because he finds a certain reassurance in the people back in Texas, especially girls; his male pals like to remind him of his background whenever he goes back there and he's even attended international PR interviews suffering from sore red marks on his face where they had ruthlessly paintballed him the previous weekend! Chace is known to be very grounded – entertainment lore tells us that it is often the stars who enjoy the most rapid rise to fame that are most likely to implode. So with Chace having gone from aspiring actor to one of the hottest names in Hollywood in a few short months, it might be harder than you think to keep a reality check. One aspect of his life that certainly helps him here is his on-going friendships with pals from his childhood. He is still very close with people who have known him when he was just a kid at summer camp trying to get his first kiss. 'I've had the same friends since school,' he told *Ladmag*, 'and they find it so weird. I went to this amazing party a while ago and asked one of my best friends, Jason, if he wanted to come along. He was totally stoked but had no way of getting there, so I was like, "No problem, I'll send my car." So this amazing car picks him up from his house and drives him across the country to an incredible manor house and the paps are going mad as he gets out of the car with flash bulbs going off all around. He was like, "Duuuudde! What *is* this?!"' When he turned 24, Chace flew loads of his old college pals up to NYC, then on to the nearby resort of Watermill by private jets where they then stayed over for a weekend-long party. They were all fed by a private chef and also chartered a speedboat and kayaks.

Chace makes no secret of the fact he still loves to visit home; every summer he returns to his grandparents' lake house north of Texas and messes about on the water with his sister and her BFFs. The only real downside to fame with his old mates is that sometimes they might be a little uneasy around his good looks! 'Some of my friends now are a bit funny when I'm hanging out with them and their girlfriends. They just give that look that says, "Chace, don't even try." They've no reason not to trust me, but they still give me that look.'

Given that only a few years earlier he was an unknown at university, it must be fairly mind-boggling for Chace to see billboards with his photo twenty feet high or read stories in national magazines and newspapers about himself, especially when many of these reports are completely fabricated, as he told *Vman*. 'If I'm standing next to a dog, they'll say we're dating. Or next to my sister – I got that as well. I let it roll off my back. There's a lot of speculation with no reality to it, complete fabrications about my private life. My close friends and my family – ha! – they obviously know what the reality of my private life is. It's just comical.'

One obvious upside of his celebrity was the number of awards he would soon start to win. Fast-forward to Season

3 of *Gossip Girl* where we find the most obvious and biggest profile accolade that Chace has won to date regarding his looks, namely the 2009 'Hottest Bachelor' gong from *People* magazine. Although the trophy might sound rather trite, it is in fact a massively influential poll and previous winners have generally enjoyed great publicity as a result (*American Idol* winner Taylor Hicks, Matthew McConaughey and Mario Lopez are three examples). The award came with a front cover feature too and was a very high-profile recognition of Chace's new-found fame. Teasingly, he ambiguously told the magazine that, 'I'm not *not* looking for a girlfriend – but I'm not particularly looking for a girlfriend, either.'

Despite his modesty, he was openly thrilled by the award. Speaking to Ryan Seacrest on the latter's KIIS-FM radio show, Chace said, 'We were trying to watch the college games last night. Me and my friends are flipping through and [on] *Access Hollywood*, they're like x-ing out the other guys. When they're x-ing out [George] Clooney, that's when it hit me. I go, "Wow, that feels pretty surreal."' Chace also revealed that he had only told his parents in advance about the award: 'It's such a big deal. It's funny I didn't really realise how massive [it] was going to be.' He has won other relatively prestigious awards too, such as the Teen Choice Award for 'Breakout TV Star' in 2008.

And just how did this 'hottest bachelor' maintain his fabulous physique? 'I'm a big gym frequenter,' he told blockbuster.co.uk, 'I guess I got it from playing sports in Texas. I played football from fifth grade onwards so working out was part of my lifestyle. My sister is a personal trainer and my dad and mom go to the gym so it's kind of a family thing. It's a way of life, a lifestyle.' Mind you, he seems to have to work hard at not eating junk food, as this fun quote from the promotion of *Covenant* is anything to go by! Asked what superpowers he would most like to have and how he would use them if he was a real-life warlock like his character Tyler, he said, 'I would abuse my body and eat McDonald's, then use my powers to decrease the fat!' (he later retracted this opinion somewhat after watching *Supersize Me*!). That said, he also suggested, 'There would be no such thing like taxes or speeding tickets for me ever again.' He's also on record as saying, 'There's nothing sexier than a Big Mac. I don't eat a lot of them, but it's just a whole complete package.'

Even though Chace was always conspicuously grateful for the awards and props he got for his looks, he was also always a little uneasy about being taken too lightly: 'I'm trying everything I've got to struggle against that stereotype,' he modestly told the Canadian edition of *TV Guide*. 'As far as the sex symbol thing goes, I'm not ready for any of that. To be labelled that, I guess, is an honour, but it doesn't give me any sort of validation. I gauge myself when I see the work being done.'

Speaking in *VMan* he reiterated his awareness of being 'pigeon-holed': 'There are a lot of adverse effects of being a certain type, which I am. Look, I wouldn't be in the business if I didn't feel I had what it takes to have longevity. Everyone has a certain castability (sic), or quality they're always going to have to fight. I think the best remedy is to reinvent yourself. I'm not going to take the same type of role in the future.'

At times his wariness at being typecast spills over into his 'day job' at *Gossip Girl*. Referring to scenes where he takes off his shirt, he told *OK!* that,

'I like to keep it as few and far between as I can. I mean, I don't want to be a shirtless whore! I don't want to come across as a himbo – is that what you call it? But it's part of my job, it's probably going to plague me for ever. There was an episode where we were crashed out on the sofa after a big night out and they wanted me to wake up in boxers, so I argued with them about it, I mean, first of all, who gets wasted with their buddy and smokes weed and then strips down to their boxers before they pass out on the couch?! No one does that. Why am I naked on my buddy's couch? It was weird so I fought it.'

His movie idols were partly responsible for this slight reticence; Leonardo DiCaprio, River Phoenix and Paul Newman all had phases of their careers where their stunning looks threatened to choke off a variety of roles and so Chace is understandably conscious that the same does not happen to him.

It was a sign of his considerable fame that by May 2009, Chace, along with Ed Westwick, was invited to attend The

White House Correspondents' Dinner – a celebrity-drenched occasion that on that night also saw such famous faces as Ben Affleck, Eva Longoria and John Cusack among the 2,000 or so guests.

Impressively, as Chace has acclimatised himself to the white-hot spotlight of fame, he has impressively started to use his celebrity to good effect too. This is the reason he involved himself in a campaign and TV advert for teensforjeans.com and dosomething.org, a campaign designed to get people donating their old branded jeans to raise funds for homeless charities. The power of a famous face such as his can fuel donations and awareness of such charities beyond all expectations and Chace was keen to make sure that his new-found celebrity was always maximised for good causes.

It has inevitably taken Chace some time to get used to the fame game, but he doesn't complain in interviews and even when a private dinner or party is interrupted by photographers there are never reports of him lashing out or moaning about his life. This is one star who seems very happy with his success. And regardless of the ups and downs of his new fame, in just a few short months Chace Crawford had become one of the most sought after new actors on the planet.

CHAPTER 6

'Have You Met My Friend Chuck?'

2008 WAS A BUSY year for Chace as alongside *Loaded* it also saw another movie role, this time in the supernatural flick – billed as 'a tweener horror' – called *The Haunting of Molly Hartley*. The lead role of Molly was played by Haley Bennett and fellow CW star AnnaLynne McCord was also cast as one of the 'bad girls'. The film was ambitiously described by one source as '*Carrie* for the *Gossip Girl* generation', a reference to the seminal Stephen King horror flick that to this day is one of the greatest scary movies ever made.

The film opens with a shocking scene – an unknown girl is meeting her boyfriend in a wooden shack in a forest, only for her father to interrupt them and insist she comes home with him. Clearly a troubled dad, in the subsequent argument on the journey he discovers they intend to get married, but then inexplicably spins the car only for it to be hit by a huge truck. With Molly lying badly injured but still alive, her father then takes a shard of windscreen and stabs her to death, while mysteriously saying, 'I can't let you turn 18, I couldn't let them take you.'

Fast-forward to the present day and the central character of the film is a college-age Molly who is suffering from recurring and very frightening nightmares ahead of going to her expensive new private school. The film is nearly twelve minutes in before Chace's character Joseph makes his appearance, a pupil reading monotonously from *Paradise Lost*. When he smiles at Molly, it's clear from the resulting ruffles around the girls in the classroom that he is the subject of much female attention. In this role he looks very young, especially bearing in mind he is six or seven years older than his character.

While Molly struggles to settle into her new school, Joseph is one of her few allies – seemingly – although the preponderance of 'evil whispering' in dark corners suggests there is more at play here than just Molly's first-term nerves. This is reinforced by her nose bleeds and severe panic attacks – usually induced by malevolent spirits – again with Chace/Joseph as her main source of support. Chace's appearances in the film are relatively limited, usually as a smouldering shoulder to cry on.

As the film progresses we discover that Molly's mother appears to be mentally ill, and there is a particularly harrowing 'flashback' scene in the bathroom when she attacked and attempted to kill her daughter by stabbing her in the chest with a pair of scissors. Her mother was subsequently locked up as a potential paranoid schizophrenic or psychotic, and the hereditary component of these diseases plays on the young Molly's mind. For Chace's young, predominantly teenage fan base, no doubt these scenes were rather more harrowing than they were perhaps used to seeing in *Gossip Girl*!

Molly's apparitions of her mother become increasingly disturbing and she appears to be spiralling into a madness of her own. We eventually learn that Molly's parents made a pact with a mysterious 'religious nutcase' – a foil for the devil – in a hospital corridor when their unborn child was miscarried: in return for saving the newborn's life, the devil would take over her soul when she turned 18. Her parents' attempts to kill Molly are merely designed to 'save' her from a life spent in the service of the devil. Her mother reveals that this was not the only baby to have been a part of such a pact.

An escalating series of events including numerous deaths ramp up the tension as Molly's life falls apart. Molly confides in Chace/Joseph that she believes she is about to be handed over to the devil – rather than being mentally ill and deluded – and he offers to take her away from it all, looting his father's safe deposit box and eloping. Chace's role never really progresses much beyond the handsome male love interest … until the climax of the film when it is revealed that he too is in league with the devil. In theory, being presented with a birthday cake near to midnight on your 18th birthday by Chace Crawford would normally be a pleasant surprise, but in this case he is standing next to a large knife and is soon accompanied by numerous dark shadows, representing equally corrupt souls. Some people might say that Nate Archibald was equally evil at times, although perhaps Chuck Bass would have been a fairer comparison! The film ends with her bleeding father being dragged in only for Molly to be offered the chance to kill him to redeem the situation and break the pact; instead she stabs herself, but it's too late as the clock has passed midnight. Her suicide attempt fails, she cannot be killed and the devil has won her soul.

Disappointingly, Chace has no dialogue in the film's big climax when the 'reveal' is made that he too is an acolyte of the devil, instead he stands in the shadows looking gorgeous but saying nothing. The film closes with Molly in a mental ward but she is visiting her father, not as a patient herself. She turns her back on him and walks away for ever, later to be seen as a teacher inspiring a new intake of pupils ... who are all blissfully unaware that their mentor works for the devil.

Part of Chace's motivation to take the role was a desire to find a film similar to *American Beauty*, which he rates as one of the greatest films ever made (and his own personal all-time favourite). 'I want to do the edgy independent movies, like DiCaprio did,' he told *VMan*, 'but you have to balance it out,' he says. 'It's about carving out your leading-man role. *Fight Club*? Yes! *X-Men*? Yes! All sorts of different films. *American Beauty*? Yes!' He is also a fan of cool directors such as Cameron Crowe, Quentin Tarantino and Martin Scorsese.

The Haunting of Molly Hartley employed many staple horror movie tricks such as unseen 'screeching' evil spirits, scary dreams and flashbacks, hand-held distant footage etc. and was not perceived by most critics to have broken any new ground. The characterisation was criticised as formulaic and the screenplay derided too. Notably, for the movie's promotional poster, Chace's face was bigger than any of his co-stars'. Released suitably at Halloween, the movie was received well by only a handful of critics; however, the majority were less than charitable. Blog.moviefone.com said, 'It's as if the filmmakers sought to strip the story of every possible nuance and make something that was truly generic. I've read fortune cookies that were scarier, not to mention smarter and more interesting.' However, similarly to *Loaded* before it, *The Haunting of Molly Hartley* had a very limited commercial impact – although this time the film was released to cinemas, it was in a small number only and soon after went on to DVD.

Despite his best efforts, some critics pointed out that Chace was already playing very similar roles each time: teenage hunks, usually not the alpha male types, slightly shy, often troubled. Of course he also played drug dealers (!) but again there was an element of the troubled soul even there. For *The Haunting of Molly Hartley* he was in a private school uniform, so the 'stereotype' comment was even easier to make. For

Chace, this was another disappointing film project; he still seemed to struggle to land a role in a movie that won the critics' and public's hearts.

With *Gossip Girl's* success continuing unabated, Chace and Ed became closer friends – swapping jokes at press junkets, going out on the town together and generally living the highlife as two 20-something men would.

Realising they hit it off so well, they decided to share an apartment – which of course the fan sites loved. It was a practical decision as much as two mates moving in together: not knowing whether *Gossip Girl* would have longevity as a show it made sense for the two to rent rather than buy.

Chace has since explained how the idea came about: 'We'd hung out a little while filming the pilot,' he explained to *People*, 'and we talked about it. So I called him up when he was back in London and said, "Hey, man, do you want to do this rooming thing?" He'd never lived away from home before. I had to tell the kid how to work a laundry machine!'

Chace says they lived together like brothers, arguing occasionally, drinking beers and playing pool, partying, and watching a lot of TV on a massive flat screen. He found the interest in the famous pair's intimate household habits rather bemusing; amidst rumours that the apartment was seeing its fair share of celeb parties and wild times, he said that: 'I don't know why anyone wants to read about the condition of our apartment. It cracks me up … We have a few roof-deck parties from time to time, but that's all.' (If you had been invited to one of their parties, the music on the iPod would have included mainly rock such as Nirvana, the White Stripes, Audioslave, the Black Keys, The Racounteurs, Van Halen, Red Hot Chili Peppers and Guns N' Roses as well as a fair few Brit bands such as Kooks, Stereophonics and Oasis.)

Rumours circulated that Westwick and Crawford were especially messy but this was something that Chace denied strongly, saying this had come from people who'd not even set foot in their flat. 'Personally I'm obsessive-compulsive about the placement and cleanliness of my things,' he revealed to Christopher Bollen. 'But I'm not always the best, so I had a housekeeper come every two weeks. It was pretty immaculate, I have to say. It had its down points, but Ed and I ran a good ship there for a while.'

Living with an Englishman meant Chace found himself using various British phrases, such as 'rubbish' for garbage and 'garage' too. One of Chace's best friends is from Brighton so he was already pre-disposed to the accent! Funnily enough, the two hadn't hung out much during the filming of the pilot because Ed's girlfriend was staying over with him. But as soon as the main series started, they became pals and roomed together, and things changed: 'We went for it. You kind of become brothers in that sense. And we're going through a similar craziness of the show. We don't have the same hours – it's not like we have the same 9-to-5 job every day and work in the same cubicle! It's very lop-sided, in fact. It's a good situation and it's worked out well.'

Inevitably, and perhaps farcically too, their close friendship led to entirely incorrect and rather bizarre rumours that they were having a sexual relationship – something that Chace (and Ed!) strenuously denied but which still made him laugh with bewilderment. *Gossip Girl* has a very large gay following, which *Out* magazine described as a 'cultural phenomenon whose early adopters weren't actually teenage girls but rather gay men trapped in arrested development or seeking to vicariously prolong their youth.'

As major leads in the show and with the help of their stunning looks, clearly Ed and Chace had strong gay followings too and both had been interviewed by numerous gay and lesbian publications. And of course living together in that Chelsea, New York apartment together (an area which some publications called the ('"Gayborhood" of NYC') was also noted by some magazines. But *none* of the above suggests in any way that they are gay themselves! Chace told *People* magazine how the two friends were totally bemused and eventually became indifferent to the gossip: 'You know what we really did the first time we heard it? Ed goes, "Oh, did you hear that rumour about us being gay?" I was like, "Yeah, man." He starts laughing and we're kind of like, "Okay, you want to go play pool and have a beer?"'

Chace had always known that as his fame grew, so too would public fascination with his private life and therefore the chances of such rumours circulating began to increase. After all, this wasn't the only time that 'gay' rumours had been spread about Chace. In 2008, he and former *NSYNC boy-band star JC Chasez were also moved to dismiss the rumours that they were having a relationship. 'I don't care about [people's] assumptions or anything,' a clearly riled JC said to *People*, 'but when people outright lie, that's wrong. So I think that part of the rumour is outright stupid.' The apparent reasoning was that they had been photographed hanging out at Elton John's party and also one time in Las Vegas; Chace pointed out that 'I've probably hung out with JC three times in my entire life!'

As he often does, Chace dealt sublimely with the false rumours and used his modesty and humour to ridicule the ludicrous gossips; talking to *Details* magazine he laughed off the suggestions thus: '[I'm a] model turned actor, dime a dozen, eye candy, doesn't know what he's doing ... and Perez Hilton says I have "gayface". So on top of everything else, I have to overcome gayface.' He's also said that in a way you haven't really 'made it' until someone suggests you are gay and revealed that his very first thought when he heard the gay rumour was, 'That's a stretch!'

Interestingly, while he laughed off the gay rumours, there were other whispers about his fellow cast members that he was far more seriously disgusted with. After tabloid reports that certain *Gossip Girl* actors and actresses were divas and that the cat-fighting on set was out of control, Chace was clearly angry: 'It couldn't be more opposite from the truth. We really have a wonderful cast of actors … there are no big egos, so that sorta nonsense irks me, because it detracts from who they are as real people.'

In 2009, the two pals decided it was finally time to get their own places. 'Frat time's over,' Chace told *People*, 'I needed my own space. [My new flat is] a little bit secluded and I like that … I have my own privacy … I found a nice Chipotle in the neighbourhood and that's all I need. I need my Chipotle and my little coffee maker and I'm good.'

Chace plumped for an apartment in the more low-key (and less touristy) financial district of the city. He revealed that he'd started buying minimalist leather furniture, a huge flat-screen TV and had ordered an espresso machine; he was looking forward to buying cool art for the walls and he also wanted to install a beer tap, preferably for Bud Light. Notably, when he finally made the move, his mum travelled up to NYC to help him out!

CHAPTER 7

The Celebrity Circus

SEASON 2 OF *GOSSIP Girl* is Chace/Nate's 'cougar' time, when it is revealed that he's been dating a much older woman. This led to hundreds of questions in interviews with Chace about whether he would consider a relationship with someone more mature. He was always diplomatic, perhaps aware that many *Gossip Girl* fans were of older years too! It also highlighted the increasing risk of fans and the media blurring the lines between fact and fiction, with the gay rumours and his cougar tastes all mixing up in the crazy whirlpool of Chace's ever-increasing fame! It wasn't just Chace either – the media were constantly trying to suggest that behind the scenes was just as gossip filled as in front of the camera. After all, with so many good-looking actors and actresses on board for the show, there were bound to be rumours about who was getting on particularly well with whom. Then there were the actual public relationships such as Ed Westwick and Jessica Szohr, which only whipped up the frenzy even more. Chace was regularly cornered about this 'on-set romance' question, but always seemed to wriggle out of a straight answer with some dignity! Usually he'd do so with humour, with quotes such as, 'I just hate everybody [on set], I'm just a loner!'

The second season also sees Nate's money cut off as his father has fled the country, but his lower income did little to quell Chace's growing popularity – if anything his financial predicament made Chace/Nate even more popular with his ever sympathetic fans. Again, Nate sometimes behaves in a way that if it were Chuck we would all be fuming, but somehow his character gets away with it due to his brilliant white smile and All-American beauty: when Dan takes him in and offers him a bed, his kindness is (inadvertently) thrown back in his face when Nate kisses Dan's sister Jenny. Not an ideal way of saying thanks to a good Samaritan but Nate seems to be able to act like this and get away with it!

Nate's friendship with Chuck is strengthened in this season too, but this is soured again later when Blair and Nate reconcile (once more!). And Nate's way of proving to Chuck and his recent belle Vanessa that he isn't in a relationship with Blair? He restarts his affair with Blair!

By the end of Season 2, Chace was a major TV star and *Gossip Girl* seemed unstoppable. Ever hungry for more success and always ambitious, Chace continued with an array of other projects unrelated to Nate Archibald's latest activities. One such project was a remake of the 1984 smash movie *Footloose*, which had originally starred Kevin Bacon. The tale of this

Chicago boy who inspires a town where music and dancing are illegal was a massive smash on its original release; the story was very loosely based on a real-life town in Oklahoma and Bacon's energy, fantastic dancing and on-screen charisma won over audiences around the globe. It has since been widely acknowledged as an iconic 1980s classic movie.

The original film had 'broken' Kevin Bacon as a worldwide star; it also starred Sarah Jessica Parker in one of her earliest film appearances and Madonna had even auditioned for the role played by Lori Singer – so it was clear that history suggested this film could turn an unknown or moderate star into a mega-star.

In the production chair for this re-make was Kenny Ortega (who was the man behind *High School Musical*), with shooting originally scheduled to start in March 2010. However, the film would become plagued by casting problems and delays. As well as a switch in director and scripts, there would be changes in key acting personnel too.

High School Musical heart-throb Zac Efron was initially lined up for the lead role of Ren McCormack – which would have given the project a global following immediately due to the multi-billion dollar success of *HSM* – but he eventually pulled out, with rumours suggesting he was concerned about being typecast so early in his career. After this news broke, speculation as to who would fill Kevin Bacon's dancing shoes was rife and it was perhaps a sign of his exploding fame that Chace's name was mentioned as a favourite. One rather fantastic rumour suggests that a key Hollywood executive asked his daughter about Chace taking over the lead role and her squeals of excitement and swooning over his name convinced them to approach the *Gossip Girl* hunk. For the successful audition, Chace sang the film's iconic signature tune with just a piano for accompaniment. Chace later revealed it was a very rigorous audition lasting over five hours!

Speaking to *Entertainment Weekly*, Chace said of the development: 'I know Zac and we're actually friends. He's gotta make the best choice for his career at this point and I have to make the best for mine and luckily it worked out for both of us.' When Chace was announced as the potential lead male, it seemed a very popular choice, with message boards and chat rooms delighting in the fact. Even Kevin Bacon's wife Kyra was openly pleased: 'We're thrilled! [Our daughter] Sosie is a big fan. We met him at the White House Correspondents' Dinner. Kevin and he had a chat. He's very sweet.' Her husband Kevin was quoted as saying he was really 'looking forward' to seeing Chace's efforts too. Those worried that Chace would have to wear very tight leggings and 1980s-style cut-off sweatshirts needn't have been concerned as the movie was a very modern update on the classic film.

Ahead of the first day of filming, Chace and the film's producers scheduled in nine months of intense preparation. As with *Covenant*, the physical demands of the new film were bound to be substantial and Chace happily admitted the early work was already proving very demanding: 'I've started prep for [the film] and I'm extremely sore! I've been training for days, but I'm extremely sore … It's really intense. We're getting the gymnastics and doing some workouts. I'm learning some basic moves. I've got a little rhythm. I'm realising every day how much of all the nine months [of prep] I'm going to need.' As well as the obvious physical workouts and dance training (classical and modern such as break-dancing), Chace began two hours of daily martial arts training, as well as masses of stretching and gymnastics techniques. His core strength and flexibility were the key issues and as a result within a few weeks of training, his already toned physique was starting to look even more ripped. 'I'm getting muscles that I didn't even know were there!'

When a few critics raised eyebrows that a 'non-dancer' was going to play a role that was clearly technically very demanding, Chace confidently brushed these worries aside, with his tongue planted firmly in his cheek: 'There's this bar in New York City on the Lower East Side called the Darkroom,' he cheekily told *People* magazine. 'They have the best music, so a lot of us will go down there and just kind of let go. I've got some movement!' He was also happy to put his faith in the executives who had picked him: 'It's a risk because there are such high expectations for it. One of [them] produced the original movie and they also did *Chicago* so I'm kind of trusting them and listening to whatever they say.'

In a lengthy and very insightful chat with Christopher Bollen of *Interview* magazine, Chace seemed unfazed by the challenge ahead: 'I am confident because I knew I had rhythm – and I'm athletic. I know I have rhythm, I have it in my brain. And I'm a quick learner. I'm better at doing something by imitation than being told. So if I'm working with the dance coach who tries to explain it, I say, "Just do it and I'll get it." That's how we've been working. I'm taking these private lessons. It's been unbelievable.' Mind you, what many fans didn't know was that way back when he had started taking acting lessons, his mum had suggested he also take dancing lessons, but he only went to one class before vowing never to return! As for the vocal demands of the role, Chace was also unperturbed: 'I'm a habitual car singer,' Crawford told *Wonderland* magazine. 'I actually go karaoking all the time, We get pretty competitive.'

As it turned out, however, Chace wouldn't need any further prep after all because in early April 2009, it was announced that he was no longer going to play the lead role. The reason given was simply that with the huge success of *Gossip Girl* showing no signs of letting up, Chace simply wouldn't have the time to fulfil both roles. The original plan had been to fit the filming in between seasons three and four of *Gossip Girl* but ultimately this proved impossible (the film's director Kenny Ortega would also later withdraw from the Paramount movie). Chace's would-be co-star, *Dancing With the Stars* beauty Julianne Hough, finally starred opposite Kenny Wormald when the film was shot in the autumn of 2010, with the film set for a late 2011 release.

A much smaller but nonetheless fun little side project came along for Chace in early 2009 when he appeared in a video for a song by Brit singing sensation Leona Lewis. Chace's manager knew the manager of the British star and this led to another interesting little role for him after they all hooked up at a party in London while he was promoting *Gossip Girl* in the UK. Chace and Leona had bumped into one another on a number of occasions and become friends, so when she was in New York filming the video for her next single – 'I Will Be' – she just asked Chace outright if he'd like to appear. 'She's such a sweet girl and I love her music ... and there were [originally] no lines or anything, so it was more of a favour.'

The chanteuse had taken America by storm with her multi-platinum-selling album *Spirit* in 2007. In the ballad's promo, Chace played Leona's boyfriend. Filmed like *Gossip Girl* in the Big Apple on an icy cold December day, the pairing obviously attracted a lot of publicity – surely the whole point?! – and Chace really enjoyed himself. As it happened, Chace's character did have some dialogue at the start of the video as the two stars are seen in a car anxiously holding a bag, presumably filled with money, while police sirens and the noise of New York provide the background soundtrack. Leona tells him to leave, saying she can't stay and promising to meet him later, shoving the bag into his hands and pleading, 'Trust me, take this and go!' It's not exactly a fast getaway, however, as

Leona then sits on the bonnet of their car to sing a few lines of the first verse while Chace sits in the back, probably wondering if he's going to get arrested after all. However, all is well for Chace as Leona is clearly sacrificing herself so that he can escape, and she is later seen being accosted by an NYPD officer (played by Cedric Darius).

Of course, the rumour mills swung into action and suggested that the two were an item but this was just plain wrong; Chace was only on set for a few hours and when asked if he still hung out with Leona, he answered with a rather curious phrase, saying they were 'semi-friends'. Leona told the media that she turned down the chance to kiss Chace in the video because she didn't want to upset her long-term boyfriend. Rather splendidly, she was also reticent on whether Chace would be her 'type', telling *Sugar* magazine that, 'He needs roughing up a bit! He'd be a really pretty girl … He's so beautiful, I mean, look at him. But I just don't think of him like that.' For his part, he said they were good platonic friends and as Leona is not an actress, he could see how any kissing sequence could make her feel uncomfortable.

Of course, by now Chace was hot property and whoever he worked or partied with was bound to find themselves the subject of media gossip. The false rumours about Leona were not the first time Chace had seen his relationships plastered across the front pages. Back in the autumn of 2007, when he'd been seen out on the town with *American Idol* winner and country music singing sensation Carrie Underwood, the Hollywood rumour mill had swung into full action.

Carrie had won the huge reality show then gone on to become one of the world's biggest country and western singers, scooping multiple trophies and selling millions of records. Around the time she was linked to Chace, she'd also been open that she was in the mood for dating, having broken up with Dallas Cowboys star quarterback Tony Romo (who would later become engaged to Chace's sister Candice!): 'I'd like to have someone other than my mom to call when I have good news.'

Initially both parties remained tight-lipped about any relationship. Take this non-committal quote from Carrie: 'He's really cute. I've met him and he seems like a really nice guy. He's got cool hair, he's a nice height and he just has beautiful blue eyes.' For his part, Chace was on record as saying that he'd never watched *American Idol*!

When Carrie appeared on the *Ellen De Generes Show*, she responded coyly to questions about Chace saying that she would certainly make him some home-cooked food but only if she could get hold of his telephone number first! And she topped that off by saying that she would 'cook for anyone that would like me to cook for them.'

A month later it was Chace's turn on the same show and he too was grilled by the immensely likable host De Generes. She trumped the awkwardness with Carrie by screening a naked photo of Chace ... albeit when he was a baby! But Chace was far more uncomfortable when she then produced a photo of him with Carrie, visibly squirming before neatly ignoring her probing question altogether and saying rather feebly, 'I am trying to get a pet right now.'

Unconvinced, the tabloids started to trail the couple's nights out, following them to celebrity haunts such as Manhattan's Marquee nightclub, Justin Timberlake's restaurant Southern Hospitality and Gramercy Park Hotel's ultra-trendy Rose Bar. At the latter, an unnamed source said, 'At one point, they were holding hands, off to the side of the table, like they didn't want people to see.' Only four days after Chace had squirmed on Ellen's couch, they were seen out clubbing again at the Marquee – notably dancing closely in full view of the rest of the clubbers.

The media interest meant that anything they ate at a restaurant would be listed on the Internet within hours of their meal – so we know that at Timberlake's restaurant they chewed through barbecued wings and Grannie's Pecan Pie while drinking Bud Light; if he was seen supporting Carrie's own career, such as at the side of the stage during the filming of *Live With Regis and Kelly*, again it was on the web within minutes; when their co-stars were involved in their own PR for various projects, questions about the 'celebrity couple' would inevitably arise; each time they headed out on the town their clothes were analysed in minute detail, such as Carrie's 'jewel-embellished blue dress' or Chace's 'suit and skinny black tie'.

But then, after just over six months, the news started filtering out that the two stars had broken up – and rumours said it had all been terminated by text message (which in light of the *Gossip Girl* way of life seemed entirely appropriate). However, although the two friends confirmed the break-up, the 'text dumping' was a detail that Chace strongly denied. The *Extra* TV show had quoted Carrie as saying 'It was completely mutual. We broke up over text so … it's like "peace out".' Chace just laughed this off, saying it wasn't that simple. 'No one breaks up by text! … It was all absolutely misrepresented,' asserted Chace, and went on to deny that the pair had never spoken since. The pressures on the relationship of her constant travelling on tour and also both their very active and hectic schedules is thought to have been a major contributing factor to the split.

Speaking in April 2008, Carrie told *People* that, 'We've parted ways. I actually haven't spoken to him in over a month.' There were rather conflicting reports saying it was Carrie who 'broke' Chace's heart but also that it was the actor who had decided to break it off. Chace had flown to visit her, even been spotted at dates on her tour, so he was clearly very keen. In January though, Carrie had downplayed the relationship seemingly, when she said, 'I'm not serious with anybody.'

Speaking to his sister Candice, *People* magazine reported how Chace was doing in the immediate aftermath of the break-up from Carrie: 'He's doing okay through this whole ordeal. He was upset about the break-up. It's always hard when you lose a relationship.' She went on to say that he and Carrie were still very good friends and the fact that there appears to have been no animosity is reinforced by Candice saying she thought Carrie was 'a doll'.

Reflecting later on the high-profile relationship, Chace was clearly shocked by the level of media interest in their partnership. 'I wasn't ready for all that craziness,' he later told *New York* magazine. 'I didn't realise what that was going to entail.' He elaborated on this in another interview saying, 'I have nothing bad to say about that experience. It was awesome. I just didn't know how to deal with it. I learnt a ton about dating someone in that kind of spotlight. It was such a whirlwind, but no regrets.' Carrie was similarly philosophical: 'I'm good alone for a while. It's been a while since I've just been single and free.' Chace also said that he was busy dating his punch bag and getting into spectacular shape for work!

If Chace thought the end of his relationship with Carrie Underwood would mark the end of the media and public's interest in his private life, he couldn't have been more wrong. His profile was now so high that any girl he was seen out on the town with became an immediate source of speculation. This aspect of his fame and good looks meant that he soon became 'linked' to literally dozens of women, often celebrities whom he had merely met at a premiere or party only once! It was a trickle at first, but soon it became almost a hobby to link Chace with any number of hot females – Lindsay Lohan, Taylor Momsen, Emma Roberts, Kim Kardashian for example (all denied). In interviews he would constantly be asked which celebs he found hot – some of his answers surprised a few people, such as saying he found Sarah Palin very attractive! Conversely, one fan told a reporter that she thought supermodel Cindy Crawford was his mom! More often than not this was all just mischievous reporting; for example, the 'date' with Kim Kardashian was a rumour that spread after the two had co-presented an award at a ceremony and apparently 'hit it off'. There was nothing more to it than that.

Perhaps predictably there was also talk of on-set romances, with Leighton Meester being 'linked' to Chace, something that was again denied by both parties. While denying any alleged romance she was happy to point out how good their friendship was: 'I'm really close to Chace. We're really good friends. [Along with] Nicole [Fiscella], who plays Isabel on the show. We're all just really happy people. We have the same views on life.' She went on to suggest that many of these rumours are the result of a blurring of the lines between fact and fiction: 'The biggest thing I've noticed is they kind of want everybody to be their character. Like Leighton [dating] Chace, and me and Blake hating each other. Those are our characters on the show – that's not us in real life.'

Chace muddied the waters himself though when he revealed some of his own techniques for getting close to a girl; given that he'd previously dismissed various rumours of relationships by saying a particular girl in question was 'just a friend', quotes such as the following only served to confuse! 'I try to get to know the girls I'm attracted to without having an official "date". I keep it light, become their best friend and hold off on the romance. If you're friends first, the rest of it happens more naturally.'

So what sort of girl would Chace like to date and how exactly would he go about it? Cooking seems to be the food of love. 'I love to cook,' he told MediaBlvd.com. 'I can make a mean spaghetti. I try to eat healthy – egg whites and all that.' He's also reported to be a dab hand at barbecues but also thinks if a girl brought a McDonald's to a date he'd be impressed! 'All you need is a pool table, beer, an electric jukebox and good conversation,' he once told *People*. One of the best dates he has been on was with a girl who wanted to go camping so they packed the car, drove to California and stayed for five days. Or perhaps he will find love on the golf course? 'It'd be nice to get old and have someone to play golf with.' He'd certainly be impressed if his date wanted to go to see his favourite teams the Dallas Mavericks or the Cowboys too!

Perhaps this gives a hint as to his long-standing love for Texan girls who obviously still hold a special place in his heart: 'Being around Texas girls all my life, that's what I'm used to. Maybe it's their charm, the way they're raised, their decorousness ... and that's taught me a lot about what I'm gonna want from a girl eventually. I'm using a French phrase to describe a Texan girl but they have a ... *je ne sais quoi*.'

Top tips on what to avoid on a first date are: 'an obnoxious laugh, swearing like a sailor, bad breath, breaking wind, getting blackout drunk, talking about your exes. It's a long list!' He thinks women worry too much about love handles, that there's too much pressure on them to be super-slim and he does think that everyone has 'a handful' of soulmates out there. For him, the single biggest draw would be a girl who makes him laugh. He has teasingly said he has 'experienced' love at first sight, but gives no further details.

He is certainly the romantic: 'Being romantic is subjective,' he told *Cosmo*. 'I think it's more about being creative; going outside the box. I don't do anything formal but I love to draw pictures for a girl, or take her to a concert. I don't do cheesy chat-up lines.'

Chatting up a girl now is riddled with complications too – Chace's fame has a downside in this respect in that he finds that he's not always certain about a girl's intentions when they meet. As a result, he is more cautious about new relationships.

He has even joked that he might be better off dating anonymously online. Given his massive internet fan base and the huge number of chat rooms and forums dedicated to Mr Crawford, one can only imagine the thrill this statement sent around the world of online Chace lovers!

Seriously though, this aspect of fame doesn't worry him because he is in no rush to settle down; he cherishes the idea of a loving wife and kids at some point in his life, but for now he is clearly enjoying his 'hottest bachelor' status, something that is not about to change. When he does finally get hitched, he wants two or three kids, a couple of dogs and a big house near a lake, but Chace fans might have to wait a while yet to pop the question: 'I don't trust myself to get married in my twenties,' he candidly told *People*. 'I don't feel like I'm mentally there yet; right now, I'm having more fun than most 23-year-olds should be allowed to have! I'm not in any rush.'

CHAPTER 8

Not Exactly The West Side

WHILE CHACE'S PERSONAL LIFE was being pored over by the media, so too was that of his character in *Gossip Girl*, as the show became ever more popular. In Season 3 the 'nearly there' love affair between Nate and Serena reignites, and yet our man Chace/Nate is still never quite able to get sorted! This time as the ill-fated pair are about to kiss (again) they are interrupted and Nate is left heartbroken once more, only for Serena to do exactly the same again shortly after … two rejections for the price of one. By now Chace/Nate fans were painfully sympathetic to their hero's woes. In interviews, this sympathy is often visible in the way that journalists talk to Chace – friendly, kind, slightly patronising sometimes, whereas with Ed/Chuck they talk much more directly, and even with some caution! Still, in this third season Nate wins the day and eventually, in Episode 13, he and Serena finally become a couple! The cheer that went up around the world was almost audible when this finally happened. It's short-lived, however, and before the season finale Serena has broken it all off again. Scorned, Nate closes the season with two women on his arm. His fans were thinking: *Yes, but that's not what he really wants …*

What Chace Crawford really wanted in real life was to keep extending his movie career. His work rate showed no sign of letting up when he took a role in yet another movie, this time in the Joel Schumacher directed *Twelve*, based on the Nick McDonell novel of the same name (which the author wrote when he was just 17). A new street drug called Twelve – a drug said to be an instantly addictive cross between cocaine and ecstasy and favoured by socialites who would not be out of place in *Gossip Girl* – has led to the deaths of several people and the film follows the drug's path of destruction as it demolishes the lives of many people, some metaphorically and some literally. Chace's character is called White Mike, an impoverished Harvard student and son of a rich restaurant tycoon who postpones his university career to sell illicit drugs to his former classmates, so a somewhat different personality to the squeaky-clean and privileged Nate Archibald that he had become so well known for! (Some sources had Schumacher himself describing the film as '*Gossip Girl* on steroids'.)

Chace himself described White Mike as 'dark, serious and tragic', although it is worth noting that Mike himself does not use drugs or alcohol. In the film his character's mother had died one year previously and he was struggling to cope with the loss and his empty life, not least because her illness had financially ruined his family. His suppressed grief and sense of alienation from much of the world underpins large segments of the movie's plot and Chace's acting out of this painful sense of loss is acute and striking.

In this movie, Chace's character is the lead male, with much of the opening section of the film centering on him. Many of the key scenes in the movie revolve around or heavily involve his character – the murder of his cousin, various drug deals, a fateful confrontation with the drug Twelve's supplier (Lionel, played by 50 Cent), the climactic shoot-out at a party and the emotional closing scenes with his co-star Dionne Audain. Promotional posters would also feature Chace as the largest star, dwarfing the pictures of his co-stars such as 50 Cent and Emma Roberts.

Chace threw himself heartily into the major role, not just technically but physically too. Tabloid paps and even fans gossiped about how much weight Chace had lost – a physical transformation that was required for his drug dealer persona (some reports had the already lithe actor losing over a stone). He lived as a 'hermit' for weeks to strip the fat off him and also to take on the troubled persona of his character. Even his famously unblemished skin seemed to be pale and puffy, and he was often seen on set looking very scruffy and dishevelled – so much so that in between takes he found he could stroll around New York and no one even recognised him, quite a difference to the traffic jams he would cause when he was filming as Nate Archibald! He admitted he loved being incognito again. And the weight loss and less obvious 'pretty boy' looks reassured him that he could avoid that dreaded 'hunky' stereotype that he seems so sensitive to. That said, his character was still swirling around the Upper East Side of Manhattan's wealthy set, so in a sense there was a definite continuation from *Gossip Girl* too.

The whole atmosphere on set was also much more modest than the high-profile *Gossip Girl* circus. There was one trailer for the entire cast and a very strong sense of team spirit pervaded the whole shoot. This helped add to the dark intensity that Joel Schumacher was searching for. It was by no means all serious though – the cast often finished work and headed up to Chace's apartment where he has 'a world class roof-deck' and the party would start!

That dark intensity was helped enormously by some of the cast – most obviously 50 Cent who, as one of the biggest rap stars ever, was a huge bonus to the film's chances. Given Fiddy's own very traumatic childhood and his notorious gang experiences, some people wondered how he would get along with a southern boy who went to church and seemed to all intents and purposes to be his exact opposite. No such problems, in fact, there seemed to be a genuine affinity: 'The nice soap star, and the brutal gangsta rapper?' Chace pondered with *GQ Style*. 'Yes, yes. A supposition that it would be extremely close to potential conflict. Which of course it wasn't.

We got along just fine, I couldn't think of a better colleague. 50 Cent is a special person. And incredibly intelligent when it comes to career planning.' Chace clearly enjoyed working with the rapper and revealed a surprising soft side to the famously tough guy image: 'He's just a big jokester. [50 Cent] is like Mr Nice Guy Next Door. He gives everyone a big hug, makes sure everyone's having fun and keeps it light. I remember the day I was driving home from school and his first CD came on. I absolutely loved him, so [working with him] was pretty surreal.'

Another actor of note was the film's narrator, none other than Kiefer Sutherland who had made his own breakthrough in *The Lost Boys*, the film which Chace's first cinematic foray *Covenant* had been so poorly compared to, and which was the second so-called 'Brat Pack' film directed by Joel Schumacher (the first was *St Elmo's Fire*).

The film's director clearly made an impact on Chace; not surprisingly, perhaps, as Schumacher was one of Hollywood's most respected directors having been behind the lens for films such as those two Brat Pack movies but also blockbusters like *Batman Forever* and *Batman and Robin*, as well as successful but less commercial films such as *Flawless* and *Tigerland*. (Notably, Chace has said he would love to play the Caped Crusader in a movie adaptation and cites Val Kilmer as a key influence.)

Chace loved working with Joel Schumacher and in particular revelled in the artistic freedom that the director encouraged. Speaking to Christopher Bollen for *Interview* magazine, he said: 'It was much more of a low-key, smooth situation with Joel Schumacher running it. There were no big master scenes outside. It was more improv – just throw and go.' In the same interview he also said, 'I'm in awe of Joel. He's an artist. And he has such a vision that he makes you feel comfortable. Obviously, the role is a bit of a risk for me personally, but he gave me this confidence when he set a certain kind of tone or energy on the set. Joel's the man.'

Filmed in Chace's new home city of New York, the movie was a very edgy and fast-paced independent thriller, laced with credibility and certainly a very authentic progression in his big-screen career. The film was clearly being taken more seriously than *Loaded*, not least because its premiere was at none other than the critics' favourite Sundance Film Festival, on the last day of January 2010.

Critical reaction to Chace's new movie was mixed and box office takings were rather muted. In fact, some sources rate the box office as less than $200,000 in the first two weeks, with a global box office gross of around $2.5 million. In Hollywood terms this is not a large sum of money.

The depiction of violence and death was quite severe and some suggested that Chace's younger audience might find this upsetting, but it is ridiculous to expect him to restrict his roles to only those that satisfy the moral values of a very young fan base. This was inferred in a scathing review in the *New York Times* by Stephen Holden when he said that Chace had been 'painfully miscast'. His barbed pen wasn't reserved for just Chace, going on to say it was 'a tawdry melodrama' that was 'more interested in gaping salaciously at the depraved, joyless lives of the denizens [portrayed] ...'

Holden wasn't alone. Many critics felt the voice-over narration of Sutherland was superfluous and irritating; reviewers criticised the styling too, with the *Village Voice* saying, 'Though Crawford's bangs and facial hair are the most art-directed aspect of the movie, he's costumed to look like a member of the Trenchcoat Mafia.' *Rolling Stone* simply said it was 'a drag-ass slog'. In general, European critics reacted much more positively to Chace's part and the film itself, which suggested there might be a backlash against *Gossip Girl* in America that was colouring how people viewed Chace's latest efforts. Nonetheless, with comments like this from Wetpaint.com, it was hard to see how the new movie could benefit Chace's otherwise shining rise to fame: 'Chace Crawford (Nate) won't be winning any Oscars this year. The critics hate his new film *Twelve*. It's no shock the film was universally derided when it debuted at Sundance.'

So it was another sideways step at best in Chace's film career; however, although *Twelve* was neither a critical nor commercial hit, there was a sense that Chace was a natural on the big screen and there was a growing feeling in Hollywood that it is only a matter of time before he catches a role that will make him one of the world's biggest movie stars.

After the filming for *Twelve* had wrapped, Chace admitted that heading back to the frenzied circus that was shooting *Gossip Girl* had been something of a culture shock. 'I jumped back into *Gossip Girl* on a Monday,' he told Christopher Bollen, 'and I was so stressed the first day back. There's the first shoot of the episode on location, and it's triple the mayhem. Of course, it would die down in a couple weeks, but there were paparazzi guys flying around like wasps, completely disrespectful.'

Gossip Girl is famous for its so-called 'walk and talk' scenes, where key characters are filmed strolling along an apparently 'everyday' New York street usually having some emotionally drenched heart-to-heart. However, the reality is very different and Chace says this peculiar fact is one of the hardest and most challenging aspects of that show: 'You're walking and just talking about life and death,' he told Bollen, 'you're having a serious conversation, looking someone in the eye, but everywhere around you, it's literally a circus. Sometimes I sit back and laugh. But it definitely drains your focus and energy. I come out so mentally exhausted.' He compared the show's filming to going back to high school, in that you bump into all these people that you had been with the previous year!

By now another aspect of *Gossip Girl*'s appeal was almost as popular as Chace and his fellow actors! The fashion and style of the series has become a crucial part of its success and of course Nate and Chuck were instrumental in this. Chuck is clearly the most outrageous of the cast in terms of his clothing but Chace/Nate has developed a neat line in the most stunning designer suits and formal wear. Chace enjoys wearing the high-fashion tailored suits that Nate dons, and has increasingly been spotted in the front row of various catwalk shows, especially around Europe. Armani have in particular been very welcoming and although he claims he is no fashion or style icon as some observers would have it, he thoroughly enjoys this glamorous side of his job.

His own personal style has shifted too; notably in the pilot Nate's hair is gelled high but this was a look that did not return for the series run: 'I got them to comb it down, it was up in the pilot and wasn't me.' His floppy hair has since been mimicked by millions of boys and men around the world and even rivals that of vampirish Robert Pattinson. He tends to play down his style when asked about this in interviews: 'It's important to have a certain look in the industry but I honestly tend to wake up and comb my hair with my hands. I think I have three pairs of the same jeans, so when I find something I like, I tend to stick with it.'

Personally Chace likes more classical looks like Ralph Lauren and John Varvatos although he's also a fan of the more garish Dolce & Gabbana; 'I'm a friend of the subtle.' For a Texan native – an area that he has said is keen on the 'head-to-toe denim outfits', he certainly has some style. He told *GQ* that, 'I actually enjoy carrying a perfectly fitting suit. Because I just feel better in good clothes. Which I only know since I'm interested in cuts and styles.' Chace cites Paul Newman in *Cool*

Hand Luke as a style influence and also Steve McQueen. Notably, in real life Chace does not have a personal stylist, unlike many of his Hollywood peers, instead he chooses all his own clothing himself. He's also got heavily into luxury watches too, with premium brands such as Panerai, IWC and Audemars Piguet – which can cost five figures ... or even more.

The above reference to 'bangs' or a 'fringe' as it is known in the UK is a trademark look of Chace's, along with his eyebrows and those startling blue eyes. When he appeared on the front cover of *VMan* magazine, his gelled-back 1950s-style hair caused quite a few ruffled feathers among his online fan base who posted pictures of the cover within minutes of its release while chat rooms all debated if it was a good look or not!

Back on *Gossip Girl*, Nate's style was necessarily the subject of feverish debate among the producers and show's stylists. It was an important factual detail because any character in real life such as Nate would inevitably spend a massive amount on clothes. Nate's style has been described as 'casual chic'; the show's stylist Eric Daman is a master of his craft and his choices of clothing have contributed heavily to *Gossip Girl*'s success.

CHAPTER 9

Dark Times

WITH ANY BIG TV hit, there will always be criticism. It's impossible to please everybody and *Gossip Girl* was not immune to this problem. So by the end of the third season, with ratings up and the PR presence of the show and its lead actors and actresses never higher, there was something of a backlash against the glamorous programme. The criticism and controversy came on several levels.

Firstly, some observers criticised what they saw as an over-sexualisation of a show that was targeted at teenagers. The steamy sex scenes and relentless frolics were of course lapped up by the fans but this did not stop worried older minds expressing their concern. Writing in the *Independent*, Guy Adams gave a very balanced overview of the show and was very complimentary about Chace in particular, but did reserve judgement on some aspects of the programme:

'At the heart of the show, there lies an emptiness. Watching it can feel like scoffing fast food: it may serve a purpose, and will certainly tickle your taste buds, but you can't help worrying if it's all that healthy. Some of the show's fruitier scenes, many involving a half-naked Crawford, feel superfluous. And the storylines and values espoused by its sex-obsessed, often selfish and materialistic stars are what curmudgeons might call a sad reflection of the youth of today.'

Given the saucy nature of much of *Gossip Girl*'s storylines, Chace admitted that he was sometimes a little awkward about his family seeing the show. Having sex on a bar stool might not be what you want your mum to see, but he also revealed that his grandmother was an avid fan too, and would hold *Gossip Girl* parties with her elderly pals. On one occasion she phoned him up to chide him for the 'cougar' storyline when his character Nate went with an older woman. He joked that his granny and her friends 'represent all of the 65-and-over demograph' of the show round the entire world.

Other critics panned the 'predatory' lifestyles of the women and questioned the message this was sending out to the show's millions of female fans. Critics also derided the obviously materialistic focus of these people, the craving for possessions ahead of happiness. When some journalists called it 'a parent's worst nightmare', *Gossip Girl* – in a display of confidence in their show – simply turned this around and made it a slogan for a new set of adverts. Critics cried foul, saying they were not taking their influence seriously.

Chace admired this openness and said in the *Inquirer* that he understood some people's reservations: 'They [the show's creators] keep it edgy. That's part of the reason why our adult demographic is growing because there's a lot of adult material … [although] I wouldn't let a 13- or a 14-year-old watch the show.'

Chace himself came in for a fair amount of criticism too, sometimes exacerbated by the blurring of those lines between fact and fiction. Of course, Nate Archibald's privileged background made that character an easy target for snipers, but because Chace did not come to the table with stories of 'impoverished artist' in his portfolio, many detractors also said he'd had it too easy. He'd only been acting three years, they said, others suggested it was largely down to his good looks.

Chace had previously stated he knew the time would come when the almost universal acclaim would turn and he'd be criticised. He was ready for this and employed a sure-fire way to defuse this critical attack; his innate modesty: 'I realise how fortunate I am,' he told *Vman*. 'I had a lot of things fall into place, by chance, kind of a fluke. There was definitely a hint of good luck to it. But I do have a drive and a certain curiosity that not all people have.'

As a relative newcomer, he also finds the more pretentious side of Hollywood rather vacuous: 'There are a lot of people that try too hard to be the starving actor and to be really pseudo-intellectual and dark, when, really, there's a business side to manage and push towards.' And Chace leaves no stone unturned in proving his critics wrong – his ambitious drive is matched by a self-critical edge that means he always watches every episode at least once to check how he comes across and to spot any elements of his acting that can be improved. He finds watching himself on-screen uncomfortable but understands that this is one of the main ways he will improve.

Another problem *Gossip Girl* inevitably came up against was competition. The appeal of being the latest 'big thing' in TV-land is joyous but also by definition short-lived; for *Gossip Girl* there were soon rival shows vying for attention, such as *Criminal Minds* and *Grey's Anatomy* spin-off *Private Practice*. Some industry commentators suggested that for all the hype and massive online buzz about the show, the actual ratings were not quite as spectacular, with the first season notching up only 196th in the list of prime-time shows. Others said that the show had similarly modest ratings across the pond in the UK, so it could not be considered a truly international hit. Responding to this, Chace said, 'To be honest it's almost a blessing in disguise that it's not some massive mega *90210* that typecasts us and goes a decade. It's a bit more under the radar and cult in a way. I'm sort of fortunate for that.'

With so many good-looking and highly ambitious actors and actresses on set, it was also perhaps inevitable that rumours of catfights and squabbling started to surface. Speaking to the *Daily Goss*, Chace simply shrugged his shoulders and denied any such problems: 'That's the funny thing, they always try and twist our private lives. They want it to be like the show with the catfights but it's exactly the opposite. After an 80-hour week we'll be in the van exhausted and we're like, "Hey what you guys doing? Do you want to grab some food?" We're all very close and we're best friends. We get along very well, surprisingly I know. I wish it was more interesting.'

Unfortunately, the difficult times were not over yet because in June 2010 Chace made headlines once again and this time it was with regard to an incident in his personal life. Given Chace's very amiable persona and reputation within Hollywood for being a likeable guy with fierce ambition and drive, it was naturally with great shock that the world woke up on 4 June 2010 to reports of his arrest. He had been charged with misdemeanour and possession of marijuana.

According to reports he'd just returned from a lovely family trip to Mexico where he had spent the Memorial Day Weekend at a luxury resort with his sister Candice and her boyfriend, American football star Tony Romo (who had previously dated Carrie Underwood and Jessica Simpson). His parents were also on the trip.

Back in Plano, Texas, police said Crawford was sitting in a vehicle with a friend in a car park outside the Irish bar 'Ringo's Pub' just after midnight when he was arrested for one count of possession of less than two ounces of marijuana. Chace immediately insisted he was innocent and was simply in the wrong place at the wrong time; the worrying fact was that if convicted, court reporters suggested he could face up to six months in jail, or a $2,000 fine or both. Reports suggested it was one unlit joint that was found in the car and not on Chace himself. Chace was not smoking the joint at the time. 'Sources' adamantly denied the joint was his.

Soon after, both Chace's mug shot and the official police arrest documents were available to view online – listing his place of residence as New York. It was very shocking to see Chace's police photo spread across the Internet and it was not lost on the watching world that his character in *Gossip Girl* is a prolific pot smoker – again blurring the lines between fact and fiction.

Attention on the case was obviously high with one camera even turning up at the McKinney, Texas courthouse when he attended to listen to the formal charges. Chace was accompanied by two men – presumably security – and was wearing a white shirt and smart tie, but otherwise it was a very low-key court appearance. When the matter came to a resolution some time later, Chace agreed to perform 24 hours of community service, report to his probation officer every month and 'maintain good conduct' for 12 months. In return the case was dismissed and he would have no criminal record.

This came as a great relief to his millions of fans – in the past few years a large number of very famous and young stars had become embroiled in drug, drink and other scandals, so it was a relief that Chace was not to be one of these. Lindsay

Lohan is the most obvious example of an actor going off the rails with a litany of offences against her, along with spells in rehab and jail; Britney Spears is another female star who has battled scandal. Chace was not about to join any such list. Despite the negative headlines of the marijuana incident, Chace is actually a clean-living boy – although he once got two speeding tickets in one night, one when he picked up his girlfriend in his seventies Dodge Challenger and one when he'd just dropped her off!

In a strange and equally innocuous parallel to her brother, Chace's sister Candice was arrested in 2007 for alleged 'underage possession of alcohol' at a bar on Columbia, Missouri. With the spotlight on her as well as her brother, Candice's love life has become the source of media attention and interest too. Since 2009 she had dated the star quarterback of the Dallas Cowboys Tony Romo and in May 2011 they were married in front of 1,600 guests. Inevitably, comparisons are made in the media between the two well-known siblings, with perhaps the most superficial and comical being 'they have the same eyebrows'. The regional publication *D Magazine* named her one of 'The 10 Most Beautiful Women in Dallas 2010'; DFW.com named her one of the 11 'Hottest people in North Texas'. It's all in the jeans (sic).

After this small stutter, Chace's stellar career was free to keep on exploding. The 'arrest' episode had certainly not affected his popularity one jot – according to one website, 'mug shot or not, Crawford still managed to look hot'.

CHAPTER 10

He's Just Getting Started ...

SEASON 4 TELLS US that thanks to Chuck's 'Little Black Book' Nate has been very busy sleeping around with numerous one-night stands. Even here, with behaviour that is not very becoming, Chace fans could forgive him; he is, after all, suffering from a broken heart! Maybe it's his stunning looks, maybe his soft demeanour, maybe it's the confusion between Nate and Chace, but whatever Nate gets up to on-screen seems to have little affect on Chace's popularity! Despite recent difficulties with the marijuana arrest and the backlash against *Gossip Girl* in certain circles, there seems to be no sign of Chace's celebrity declining.

Maybe Chace will break his 'critics' duck in 2011 with the release of his next movie project, *Peace, Love and Misunderstanding*. The independent comedy-drama is being directed by the Academy Award-nominated Bruce Beresford, perhaps best known for being behind the lens of *Driving*

Miss Daisy (which scooped an Oscar in 1990). Starring alongside Chace will be *Grey's Anatomy* actor Jeffrey Dean Morgan and Hollywood legend Jane Fonda. The film centres around a lawyer and her two children who visit their hippy grandmother at Woodstock. Chace plays a character called Cole who is billed as 'a war-protesting butcher who catches the eye' of the lead female's daughter – reassuringly this character doesn't sound too much like Chace's usual parts! At the time of writing it is unclear how substantial that role is. Much of the filming was on location in New York's Hudson Valley and was described by the *Hollywood Reporter* as 'a multi-generational indie flick'. His admiration for actors such as Leonardo DiCaprio who star in big blockbusters as well as indie films was obviously a key motivator behind Chace's decision to take the role; time will tell if it was a good call.

At the time of writing, Chace is also scheduled to star in *Responsible Adults*, a romantic comedy set to feature Katie Holmes, the wife of Tom Cruise. The movie is written by Alex Schemmer and will be directed by Jon Poll (various *Austin Powers* movies, *The 40-Year-Old Virgin*, *Dinner for Schmucks* and *Meet the Fockers*). Rumours suggest Holmes' character is a 32-year-old mum who seduces the younger man played by Chace only to find out that they'd already met many years ago when she was his babysitter! Chace will play a 22-year-old called Baxter Wood with shooting scheduled to take place in Los Angeles in late 2011.

Chace has also done some voice-over work for three episodes of *Family Guy* after meeting the show's creator Seth McFarlane at a party. On one episode, his voice was used during 'The Former Life of Brian', a reference to the famous Monty Python movie. Chace's character appears as 'a stranger at a gym' and offers steroids to the main characters who are struggling with their fitness. He also appeared on episodes called 'Stew-roids' and 'Dial Meg for Murder'. 'That,' Chace told *ES* magazine, 'was more of a dream come true than many things ... I get a good kick out of it, it's funny.' (He's also a big fan of *The Office*.)

Chace has also provided the voice for the John Connor character in *Robot Chicken*, an American stop-motion animated TV series that has a huge cult following. The show is a non-stop onslaught of popular culture references and surreal comedy, so it was a refreshing diversion for Chace to be involved. This is not mere jesting though – the 2008 'Star Wards' episode was actually nominated for an Emmy! Like many other cartoon and animated shows in the US, there is a tradition of celebrity guest voice-overs; Macaulay Culkin, Jean-Claude Van Damme, Snoop Dogg and even George Lucas have all chipped in, so Chace was in good company. The three episodes he has appeared in are called 'Cannot Be Erased, So Sorry', 'Terminator' and 'Maximum Douche'.

Any book on Chace Crawford can't be complete without a look at the similarities – and differences! – between him and the character that made him famous, Nate Archibald. It's a question that Chace is repeatedly asked in interviews and picks up again on the public's fascination between what they see on a TV screen and what a celebrity is like in real life. Chace says he does share some characteristics in common with Nate, although very much more toned down. He has never been in a love triangle, although as we've previously seen he did once date his ex-girlfriend's best friend, albeit 'way after. And no one cared, I was a dork!' Talking to *CW Source*, he happily admitted that in Nate's personality there is 'a lot of me in there as far as the emotional stuff and the family stuff.'

'I'd like to think that I have more of a sense of humour,' Chace told the *Daily Mail*, 'and am less uptight than Nate. I also lack his passion for all things navy!' Generally Chace champions Nate but he can also see his character's limitations: 'My character always takes the right decision,' he told *Cosmo Spain*, 'which can be a bit boring, right? In life you have to take risks! Nate is this undecided character, he never stops fighting for what he thinks he believes in. So we aren't alike: I'm a less serious guy, I try to take things more lightly!'

Nonetheless, he feels that on the more serious matters he and Nate do share some traits: '[We] both have a certain moral conviction in life,' he told *TV Guide*. 'At 17 there is not much else to have on your plate except what college you're going to go to and what girl you're dating or want to date. I can relate to that pressure a bit because our private school was a bit of the same. Nate also wants out. He doesn't know exactly what he wants, but he knows what he doesn't want and I can relate to that.'

Chace is also on record as saying the pressure of high school social circles is definitely something he can relate to, but when talk turns to Nate's parental pressure and his overbearing father, Chace is quick to point out how fabulous his own dad is: 'I have never felt like I don't have any limits like Nate does. His father is trying to force him down a particular path in life, and he is now starting to question his family situation, his girlfriend and his future.'

And despite their differences, Chace clearly has a very affectionate place in his heart for the character that changed his life: 'He's knows girls are attracted to him and he knows how to turn on that Jerry Maguire charm ... he steps back and realises what's right and makes right decisions but sometimes he gets drawn in and ... takes advantage of it from time to time ... Essentially he's a good guy, he's got a good heart.'

And so what next for Chace Crawford? At the time of writing he's still single and enjoying dating. He is now seeing the considerable financial benefits of his massive success and this has turned his mind to a few childhood dreams that he can now afford to fulfil. For example, he's always had ambitions to get a pilot's licence. One of his favourite movies of all-time is *Top Gun*, the Tom Cruise film about the elite US airforce squadron that was partly responsible for Mr Cruise becoming the biggest actor in the world. Being a 'Top Gun' would be Chace's ultimate job and he still watches this film at least once a month! He has credited Tom Cruise with being a major influence on his acting career – apart from *Top Gun*, he has openly said that Nate Archibald is heavily influenced by the Cruise title role in *Jerry Maguire* about an egotistical sports agent tussling with his conscience (which was a huge smash hit movie for Tom when it was released in 1996).

Perhaps the reasoning behind this 'dream job' gives some indication of where Chace wants his career to go next, because it is always film stars that Chace cites as influences rather than TV actors. Equally it is acting for films that he seems to love most, as he explained to *BuddyTV*: 'I haven't done too many of either, but I really do like working on films more. There's more freedom. Television feels a little bit restrictive, so far as the dialogue, and there's really no improv. The scenes are a little bit shorter ... So, films are kind of where my head's at ... In the future. I love the show [*Gossip Girl*] though, hopefully that lasts.'

With such a versatile range – despite critics trying to pigeonhole him – Chace seems destined to keep his profile and success going strong, even long after *Gossip Girl* has finished. With Season 5 underway and his fame showing no signs of dwindling, it seems that in time we will look back and realise that for Chace Crawford fans, *Gossip Girl* was merely the start of something very big indeed!

PICTURE CREDITS

Now flip the book to read all about Ed!

THE UNAUTHORISED BIOGRAPHY OF
CHACE CRAWFORD

THE UNAUTHORISED BIOGRAPHY OF
ED WESTWICK

GOSSIP
BOYS

THE UNAUTHORISED BIOGRAPHY OF
ED WESTWICK

LIZ KAYE

10 9 8 7 6 5 4 3 2 1

First published in the UK in 2011 by Virgin Books,
an imprint of Ebury Publishing
A Random House Group Company

Copyright © Liz Kaye

Ed cover image © Tobias Hase/dpa/Corbis

www.randomhouse.co.uk

Addresses for companies within The Random House Group Limited can be
found at www.randomhouse.co.uk/offices.htm

The Random House Group Limited Reg. No. 954009

A CIP catalogue record for this book is available from the British Library

ISBN: 978075340282

The Random House Group Limited supports The Forest Stewardship Council
(FSC®), the leading international forest certification organisation. Our books
carrying the FSC label are printed on FSC® certified paper. FSC is the only
forest certification scheme endorsed by the leading environmental
organisations, including Greenpeace. Our paper procurement policy can be
found at www.randomhouse.co.uk/environment

Printed and bound by CPI Group (UK) Ltd, Croydon, CR0 4YY
To buy books by your favourite authors and register for offers visit
www.randomhouse.co.uk

Contents

Chapter 1: Panto, Piano and Plenty 7

Chapter 2: Breaking And Entering 19

Chapter 3: Gossip Girl 29

Chapter 4: The Filthy Youth 43

Chapter 5: Movie Mania 57

Chapter 6: A Sideways Step 63

Chapter 7: His New BFF! 69

Chapter 8: On The Couch ... In The Spotlight 75

Chapter 9: The Fame Game 89

Chapter 10: Snow Storms, Bikinis and Mobile Phones . . . 99

Chapter 11: A Date With Chuck Bass 109

Chapter 12: The Future 123

CHAPTER 1

Panto, Piano and Plenty

'My brother Will was more of a devil ... though I was easily led astray!'

Ed Westwick talking about how his mellow English childhood compared to the rather more excessive lifestyle of Chuck Bass in *Gossip Girl*.

ALTHOUGH ED WESTWICK HAS lived much of his adult life in the white-hot glare of super-celebrity's spotlight, it is fascinating to note that details of his childhood are rather sketchy. Despite having been interviewed thousands of times, plus the fact that due to his fame on *Gossip Girl* his fans and the media are desperate for details of his life away from the camera, Ed chooses to keep his early years relatively private. However, there are a few facts that are clear: Ed's mother is an

7

educational psychologist while his father is a business lecturer. He is the youngest of three boys, the eldest, Guy, is some 17 years Ed's senior and the middle boy, Will, is 5 years older than his famous brother. In contrast to Ed's latterday 'bad boy' persona as Chuck Bass, he insists that the opposite was the case when he was a little boy, instead telling the *Daily Mail* that, 'My brother has always been like, "Go do it, and worry about it when you're in jail!" But I've never really been that way. If anything, I'm overanalytic.'

Also, unlike his alter ego Chuck Bass, Ed's background was far from the ultra-privileged lifestyle of the Upper East Side of Manhattan that *Gossip Girl* inhabits. Life for Ed was a modest house in Stevenage, a fairly ordinary town in the southern English county of Hertfordshire. Clearly not rich like Chuck, Ed describes his family life as 'kind of middle-class'. Stevenage is a satellite suburb of London, situated about 30 miles north of the English capital, so as he grew up Ed would have easily been able to catch a train into the city. Stevenage had boomed in the 1950s and 1960s so by the time Ed was born, on 27 June 1987, it was thriving. The town has an annual tradition of staging rock concerts in its local park so perhaps Ed's lifelong fascination with rock and roll was fuelled by these early outdoor gigs!

However, Stevenage is not exactly a modern metropolis, effectively being a grouping of quite plain estates, largely inhabited by workers on modest wages, so again it was a far cry from Chuck Bass's privileged lifestyle, perhaps best illustrated by the fact that one of Stevenage's claims to fame is its thousands of street lights and traffic roundabouts. However, despite its superficially mundane appearance, the town of Ed's birth seems to have a knack of producing celebrities! Also born in Stevenage were Formula 1 world champion Lewis Hamilton; several professional footballers such as Jack Wilshere and Ashley Young and the sculptor Harry Bates.

Ed's family was happy and very close, and whenever he speaks about his childhood he has a smile on his face even if he does not divulge much information: 'I'm close to them all,' he told superiorpics.com. 'We're a really tight-knit group … I am the baby. We're all very, very close. We're great communicators, so we get along really well.'

Ed shares his regal birthday with both Louis XII and Charles IX of France so perhaps a privileged life was destined for him after all! However, rather than going to an exclusive private school, Ed attended the local St Ippolyt's Church of England Primary School. This was one of the quieter schools in the area, with few bus services and a rural atmosphere, and to this day it retains very strong links with St Ippolyt's Church nearby. So, although not quite a rural idyll, clearly this was a very safe and secure environment for Ed to grow up in.

When Ed was six he formed his first band with his brother, called Fangs of Fury! It lasted 'about five minutes. I just sat and watched him. So we were a two-man band with only one man doing something!' Spotting his interest in music, Ed's mum signed him up for piano lessons, although for many years to come he preferred playing football. In fact, he wouldn't play much music until his late teens (of course, by then his early acting career had taken off and his whole world looked very different). Ed's since said that to keep him and his brothers out of mischief, in addition to music lessons his parents also sent them to a Saturday morning drama school from the age of six. 'Mum's not one of those stage mums. I think she sent me because I enjoyed pantomimes.' Whatever the reason, it was a seed of interest in acting that would grow into a desire for a career and would eventually change his life.

At the age of 11 Ed left his primary and graduated to the Barclay Secondary School, less than a 10-minute drive down the road. This was the very first secondary school built after the Second World War, a conflict which had ripped out much of the British heartlands with relentless German bombing campaigns. Barclays is a so-called 'technological' college so Ed would have needed to show a mastery of the sciences.

At this comprehensive, Ed's personality and confidence really started to shine and in the playground he began entertaining his friends by impersonating his favourite characters from TV and the movies. He seemed to be a natural mimic with the ability to alter his voice, something which would come in handy in later years when speaking in the US accent of *Gossip Girl*'s Chuck Bass! Ed's impersonations were so good that he would often perform impromptu shows for his parents after school.

Ed was a popular kid at school and did reasonably well in his exams. Having had his first kiss with a girl aged only six (!) his first real girlfriend came when he was 15, like so many of his school mates. Perhaps not surprisingly, given his good looks, Ed was very popular with the girls in his school!

After taking his exams at the age of 16, Ed moved on to North Herts College and it was here that his interest in acting really began to take off. He studied A levels in business, law and communication but it is clear that this was not where his passion lay. It was while he was enjoying a holiday from his A level studies in 2004 that he decided to attend a two-week summer course at the acclaimed National Youth Theatre, a revered establishment with a long history of finding and nurturing some of the finest stage and screen actors, including such famous names as Daniel Craig, Sir Derek Jacobi, Dame Helen Mirren, Daniel Day-Lewis and Orlando Bloom. Here Ed was able to soak up the history and fine-tune his fledgling acting skills and, given the snobbish disdain that many critics have for TV actors, this prestigious background at the NYT would provide Ed with an enviable degree of technical training. After the course had finished Ed was dead set on a career in acting: he'd found his passion.

At this very early stage in his career, Ed is credited with appearing in a 'production' called *Goodbye K'Life* by Nino Salithers when he was just 17, although there are no reliable sources that detail the film or its release and success. Most likely this would have been a play, as he later spoke of having had some time 'on stage' before his first movies or TV roles.

By now Ed's heart was fully set on acting as a career and with the help of contacts at the National Youth Theatre, he began attending auditions fervently and was soon rewarded with minor roles in a number of British TV shows such as *Doctors* and *Casualty*. The former was a popular but very 'safe' daytime drama-cum-soap set at a fictitious medical practice in a town called Letherbridge in the Midlands, following the lives and dramas of the staff and patients at the Mill Heath Centre. The series ran for 11 seasons and Ed appeared in Episode 915, aired on 1 March 2006, called 'Young Mothers Do Have 'Em'. He plays a character called Holden Edwards but his role is very minor. It's rather basic TV drama but, on the other hand, *Doctors* enjoyed very sizeable ratings and for several years was considered a staple show on the BBC's daytime schedule, so it was a reasonable start for the aspiring young actor.

Also in 2006 came Ed's role in *Casualty*, a BAFTA-winning weekly show on BBC 1 and the longest-running medical drama TV series in the world! The programme mixes the medical emergencies that come into the A&E department of Holby City Hospital with the private lives and personal dramas of both the staff at the hospital and the people they treat. The series actually had a reputation for high-profile guest appearances, although usually of the 'Before They Were Famous' variety, and had previously featured such stars as

Minnie Driver, Orlando Bloom and Kate Winslet. Radio DJ Mark Burrows once played the part of a corpse (uncredited) which took two hours to film as he couldn't stop sneezing!

Fortunately, Ed's role in the show was a little more lively. The show featuring Ed was Episode 520 in Season 20, called 'Family Matters' and he plays a young man called Johnny Cullin, who is in a band named Isosceles (no relation to the actual indie band of the same name from Scotland), an outfit struggling to get their big break. Ed is first seen on-screen turning up with his guitar outside a small venue, ready to soundcheck for the night's gig. He arrives on foot while the obviously more 'well-off' guitarist Rob turns up in a sports car. Ed looks cool despite his character's poverty, wearing a black and red striped top under a tight-fitting leather bomber jacket. During the band's soundcheck for their first gig, the internal tension within their ranks starts to bubble over as Rob the guitarist repeatedly talks dismissively to Johnny, refusing to lend him the best equipment or try Johnny's new songs. It is this turbulent relationship between the guitarist and singer that will eventually lead to disaster.

As the lead singer, Ed has to perform several songs on camera and he reveals he has a pretty good rock and roll voice! Unfortunately after the soundcheck – during which fireworks are set off unexpectedly – an argument between the two main members of the band boils over again. When a photographer arrives to take PR snaps, the band begin to rehearse once more, only for the pyrotechnics to backfire and fling Rob into a wall of speakers, which causes a massive collapse of the lighting rig and tons of equipment crashes down on top of the band, Ed included. The unlikeable guitarist Rob suffers most and is impaled through his shoulder by the lighting rig.

Rather comically, as the two group members lie squashed and in agony, they start to argue again over who is in charge of the band! In the event, this turns out to rather pointless, as Rob's injured shoulder suggests it's unlikely he'll ever play guitar again. The unintentional comedy continues because while the paramedics tend to Rob's spiked shoulder, Johnny/Ed quits the band and runs off, causing the lighting rig to sink even deeper into his ex-friend's arm! Inside the venue Rob has to be put on an IV morphine drip to ease the excruciating pain, while Johnny and the band's new manager have a blazing row outside. It then transpires that the new manager had set-off the onstage fireworks and that is what had caused the explosion and subsequent injuries. Ed's character returns to the venue where he has a rather forced heart-to-heart with his rival the guitarist, with the snide Rob admitting that it is Johnny who is 'the one with the talent'. Bizarrely, Johnny and Rob then have time for some more musical debate while Rob is treated for his severe injury – only for the two paramedics to suggest that the two warring musicians share the writing and musical responsibilities, like 'Elton John and Bernie Taupin'. It's all rather implausible. The script is clumsy and the actions of the characters entirely unbelievable, but Ed was keen to get all the screen time he could: 'I needed to be on set, in front of the camera.'

He was certainly good for his word: also in 2006, Ed appeared in an episode of the British TV drama *afterlife*, which follows the trials and tribulations of an academic-turned-psychic medium named Alison Mundy. Unlike the record-breaking longevity of *Casualty*, this excellent show only ran for two seasons, with Ed's appearance coming in an episode of the second run. His character is called Darren and the show opens in the immediate aftermath of a serious car crash, when Ed's character wakes up to find his girlfriend Sasha slumped, lifeless, outside the vehicle. Ed/Darren and his friends have all been drinking – Ed's character had got through five pints of cider – and he quickly realises that he is in a lot of trouble. 'Prison, papers, manslaughter,' he trembles. They all start to panic until one friend suggests they restage the crash scene with the dead body of the girlfriend at the wheel. This is clearly a flawed plan as the blood on the windscreen would have been Darren's, so any forensic investigation would have easily revealed that the driver whose head hit the windscreen had not been the dead girl.

Nonetheless, faced with either moving the dead body and faking the crash or spending a long time in jail, the friends drag the corpse into the driver's seat and attempt to make the crash look like her fault. At first, it seems their dastardly plan has worked but the guilt and panic over what they have done soon starts to erode the friends' relationships and events quickly spiral out of control. As Ed's character takes control and insists his pals do not panic any more, there are hints of the same style of domination and arrogance that would later be such a big feature of Chuck Bass, his character in *Gossip Girl*.

The friends start to have visions of the dead girl's spirit covered in blood, and even begin to doubt their own sanity, not least when they receive a phone call from her mobile. After an abortive séance, matters really get out of control. The terrible incident eventually brings them into contact with the show's lead character Alison, the medium who has spoken with the dead girl.

Ed's character is very much the driving force in the crime and cover up, and his forceful London accent fits the 'street' edge of his role perfectly. In this sense, this role is the next in line of a number of 'gritty' parts that he enjoyed in his early career. At this stage, having surveyed the way he played Johnny in *Casualty* and Darren in *afterlife*, it would have seemed most likely that Ed would find a profitable niche acting in cutting-edge films such as *Lock, Stock and Two Smoking Barrels* or *Snatch*. This career path would certainly have been something Ed would have enjoyed: although he lists the bawdy British seaside humour of the *Carry On* comedies as his favourite set of films, he has expressed a desire to play roles in Guy Ritchie-style movies. Certainly his accent and his striking, angular looks fit those films perfectly. Likewise the setting here – a grim, urban landscape of estates and low income – was an environment that several of his early projects would also feature. So who would have guessed that Ed would eventually make his fame and fortune playing Chuck Bass, an immaculately dressed Manhattan spiv with a strong US accent?

CHAPTER 2

Breaking And Entering

E D WAS NOT ABOUT to rest on his laurels; further study
visits at the National Youth Theatre strengthened his
technical prowess as an actor and he would soon reap the
benefits of his hard work. For his next career break, it wasn't
just the historic background of the NYT that helped Ed, nor
indeed the techniques that he'd learned there. Instead it was a
tip-off from a member of the NYT's staff about a forthcoming
audition for a new film project called *Breaking and Entering*.

The star of the movie was none other than Brit Pack actor
Jude Law, who would star opposite the beautiful and critically
acclaimed Juliette Binoche. Just like his *Gossip Girl* co-star
Chace Crawford, Ed's first nervous steps into film were
against the odds – he had, after all, only very limited TV
acting experience and no films under his belt at all. A feature
film was an entirely different level of work altogether. Ed
was unperturbed by this daunting fact and went to the

lengthy auditions in great spirits. His enthusiasm must have combined with his acting skills perfectly because he was delighted to be offered the role of a teenage burglar and Bosnian immigrant called Zoran. Ed was still only 18 when the filming began.

Breaking and Entering was directed by the late Anthony Minghella, who had an enviable portfolio of previous work, most notably winning a 'Best Director' Oscar for his 1996 film, *The English Patient* (which also won a BAFTA and Golden Globe). He'd also directed *Truly, Madly, Deeply* and worked on the adapted screenplay for *The Talented Mr Ripley* starring Matt Damon and Jude Law, even going on to direct operatic works such as *Madame Butterfly*. Minghella's skills extended beyond directing into screenwriting as well. So for Ed to be around such a revered name within the film business at such an early age was a massive opportunity for him. That it was a gritty, edgy drama featuring a star as big as Jude Law was even more thrilling for the teenage actor.

The film was based on an original screenplay by Minghella, a dual role he had not pursued since his directorial debut, *Truly, Madly, Deeply*. Jude Law's character Will is in a marriage crumbling under the pressure of being a caring stepfather to a daughter who suffers from behavioural problems and irregular sleeping patterns. As an architect employed to help regenerate the down-at-heel King's Cross area of London, a spate of repeat burglaries at his offices draws him into a web of crime and deceit that soon unravels at great personal expense.

Also in the cast were Ray Winstone, Martin Freeman and Robin Wright Penn so Ed was in lofty company! Playing opposite Jude Law was Juliette Binoche as the Bosnian war widow with whom Law's character falls in love. Ed Westwick's role was very minor. He's seen helping the initial burglary in the offices and making off with the stolen property before the gang head back to the headquarters of the chief in charge.

It later transpires that Ed's character is the 'clumsy' son of this sinister man. Sporting a Puma baseball cap and Adidas tracksuit, this is hardly the fashionista image of *Gossip Girl*. If anything, Ed's look is that of the English 'chav', a negative term given to a generation of delinquent youths who usually wear sports or designer brands and are widely derided for living antisocial and wasteful lives.

Visually Ed looks very young, his cheekbones are very chiselled and his skin is still youthfully unblemished. His dialogue is very limited and he speaks in a London accent despite his Bosnian heritage, the inference being that Zoran is a London-born second-generation immigrant.

When the police trace the burglars to their dismal, grey flat on a grim council estate, the main character, 15-year-old refugee Miro (played brilliantly by Rafi Gavron, who would go on to become Ed's best friend) and Ed's character Zoran make a run for it across the roof tops, using all their acrobatic *traceur* (free-running) skills that made their breaking and entering so impressive. However, Ed's character falls awkwardly and injures himself, leading to the capture of both him and Miro. Meanwhile, Jude Law's character Will has followed them back to their dingy estate flat and sees the poverty in which they live. Eventually he meets the embattled mother played by Binoche and the combination of a lack of passion at home and sympathy for the Bosnian mother's predicament tumbles him into love with this woman. In doing so, he also changes the way he perceives his own life and his job of regenerating inner cities.

The European premiere of the movie was in London's Leicester Square and there was a huge media presence, with the film's stars Jude Law and Juliette Binoche spending an age talking to the cameras. However, despite the high-profile cast, glitzy premiere and release across nearly 100 UK cinemas, the film fared quite badly at the box office, with its eventual takings in the UK being less than £1 million (and less than £10 million worldwide). Critics were mixed too; take this comment from Salon.com: '*Breaking and Entering* is so bloodless that even Minghella's best ideas come off as wan and pale. We're aware of the angst and confusion these characters suffer, and yet the movie shows us nothing so messy as real pain.' However, there were some positive reviews, such as this one in the *Chicago Reader*: 'The complicated interactions involving class and culture that ensue between all these characters remain fascinating,' while *Movie Habit* said it was 'one of the most overlooked films of the year'.

Regardless of the mixed reviews and muted box office performance of *Breaking and Entering*, for Ed Westwick, 19 at the time of its release, this was a huge film debut. Although his dialogue was limited, his performance was convincing and he looked the part. His screen time was reasonable for such an unknown name and to be cast alongside such massive movie stars was incredible. He looked fantastic, even given the poverty and life of crime that his character struggled with, again more reminiscent of a Guy Ritchie character than someone like Chuck Bass. Although not a large role, his striking looks and understated but confident performance most definitely got him noticed.

Tragically the film's director Anthony Minghella later became very ill with cancer of the tonsils and neck. He was operated on in the early spring of 2008 but a week later he died in a London hospital of a haemorrhage. So sadly *Breaking and Entering* turned out to be his very last cinematic release. When he died in the middle of March that year, his passing left Ed devastated. 'He was like a father to us on set,' Ed told journalist Claudia Joseph. 'He nurtured us and made us feel very secure, which was important because it was my first job.' Ed has explained the minute detail which Anthony used to make his cast at ease. For example, there is a scene where Ed's character is seated at a table and Anthony suggested that he pour a glass of water to make the atmosphere more natural. It worked. 'He taught me how to underplay things and make my gestures more subtle.' This attention to detail is something that Ed has since said he prides himself on observing. He has suggested that this kind of directorial assistance was afforded to the entire cast, even the vastly experienced Jude Law, a mark of Minghella's reputation. Minghella had worked in TV before his Oscar-winning film career took off, so the advice he gave to Ed about attention to detail and intimacy with his character's personality would prove to be crucially helpful when Ed would later find himself cast in one of the biggest TV dramas in the world.

Christmas of 2006 was a very busy period for the 19-year-old Ed Westwick as just 10 days after *Breaking and Entering* was released to cinemas, his second major movie project hit the big screen, this time on Christmas Day itself. The film was called *Children of Men* and was directed by Alfonso Cuarón (among many films in his portfolio, he directed *Harry Potter and the Prisoner of Azkaban*). The film was a screen adaptation of the book published by P D James in 1992. It is a futuristic sci-fi vision of what would happen if the human race lost the ability to produce new babies. Opening in 2027, no newborns have arrived for eighteen years and the reality is that the human race will be extinct within a hundred years if nothing changes. When an African woman is found to be pregnant, the very fate of the entire human race lies in her safety and successful birth of her unborn child.

Once again Ed was in revered company. Lead male Clive Owen had featured in such previous hit films as *Gosford Park*, *The Bourne Identity* and *Sin City*. Julianne Moore was the lead character's estranged partner, while the Hollywood legend Michael Caine made an appearance as the ill-fated but colourful ex-hippie called Jasper Palmer. Ed's appearance is very much a small one, playing the role of Alex; indeed, his role is so minor that in virtually every review or feature of the movie his name is not even mentioned (even on the film's official website he does not get a mention). His screen time is only a few minutes, showing Ed sitting at the far end of a very long table in the huge dining room of his wealthy father. Clive Owen's character and Ed's father are talking about the pregnant African woman while Ed's character stares intently at what appears to be a hand-held gaming device strapped to his wrist, like a futuristic Tetris. His eyes are fixed in concentration, his face twitching weirdly, oblivious to his surroundings or the conversation around him. He has a pronounced side-parting and is wearing a golfer's sweater with large collars (not unlike something Chuck Bass would sport!). His cheekbones are very striking as usual, albeit blemished by some made-up acne. His character says nothing in this scene, but is shouted at by his father to 'Take your pills!' The implication is that Alex is a mentally disturbed young man, although the film never explores this avenue much further.

The film was shot in London and during the production the awful 7/7 terrorist bombings of the London underground and buses occurred, sending the capital city into a spiral of panic and grief. Ed was working in the city daily at this point so it must have been a very peculiar experience to be so excited at the new film and yet so horrified at the events around him. Despite this tragedy, the director was able to complete the filming in the capital; only the opening sequence showing a terrorist attack on London was filmed six weeks after the terrible real-life events.

The film was premiered with suitable fanfare at the 63rd Venice Film Festival in September 2006 and on its Christmas Day release in the UK, it hit the top spot for box office takings across 350 cinemas. This was a big deal for Ed to be able to say he'd acted in a Number 1 best-selling movie at such a young age. Despite his very modest part, the reflected glory of the film had a very positive affect on Ed's still relatively thin CV. The movie was not a blockbuster success, but it still took over $35 million at the box office, a respectable amount. However, the critics absolutely *loved* the film; take this comment from critic Brandon Fibbs: 'I was entranced by this movie. Hypnotised. Spellbound. In a thrall. The final quarter of the film is nothing short of an evolutionary leap forward in film-making.'

Also, since its release, *Children of Men* has been very influential and lauded for its innovative production techniques, particularly in terms of the way it was shot, with ground-breaking use of single-shot sequences and a very deliberate restriction on special effects. Again, for Ed to be around such pioneering film-making could only be a great experience. For him to be able to point out that a film he was involved in was nominated for three Oscars and had won two BAFTAs was a great feather in his cap before he'd even left his teenage years. Yet even with this brilliant success rounding off a very busy 2006, Ed was still constantly looking for new opportunities to get in front of a camera. Maybe 2007 would bring him an exciting new project?

CHAPTER 3

Gossip Girl

B Y THIS STAGE IN his career, Ed had acquired an excellent manager who set about finding quality auditions and new scripts for his young charge to read and apply for. With both of their eyes firmly set on the big time, the manager scoured the auditions and opportunities in Los Angeles, something which the ever-ambitious Ed was very excited about. He read dozens of scripts and TV show pitches, and one in particular caught his eye – it was for a drama set in the Upper East Side of Manhattan called *Gossip Girl*. With this in mind, Ed flew out to LA and went across town to the auditions (unbeknown to him, also at the very same auditions that day was an unknown young actor from Plano, Texas called Chace Crawford).

Each of the big US TV networks receives hundreds of pitches for new shows all the time, often over 500 in one season. Of these, maybe 50–70 of the creative teams pitching are asked to provide full scripts and a more detailed idea of the development of the show. After these 50 or so are sifted, only

20 will be made into so-called 'pilots'. The pilot is a test episode to gauge audience and media reactions before the vast expense of a full series is undertaken. Sometimes a full pilot episode is filmed while other times a very rough-cast 'mini' pilot is filmed, lasting maybe ten minutes or so. Of those pilots, at best a quarter make it to production – so from those original 500 pitches, maybe 5 get the green light. And of these five new shows, only one or two survive beyond the first season. TV is a brutal business.

However, when a script or pitch comes from the team behind one of the biggest shows in recent years, the process can be a lot quicker! In the case of *Gossip Girl*, it was the brainchild of Josh Schwartz and Stephanie Savage, who (along with Joseph McGinty Nichol) were the creative brains behind *The OC*, a hugely popular teen drama set in upmarket Orange County, California. First aired in 2003, the four seasons of that show established its stars – such as Benjamin McKenzie, Mischa Barton and Rachel Bilson – as major celebrities and won a string of awards (including 'Writer's Guild of America Best Screenplay' and countless Teen Choice Awards). *The OC* was even sold on to be broadcast in more than 50 countries worldwide, making it a huge global success. More relevant to *Gossip Girl* perhaps, *The OC* had its own fanatical following, largely across the Internet, with hundreds of chat rooms, forums and blogs debating the ins and outs of the relationships on screen as if they were real life. It was an Internet phenomenon as much as it was a TV hit.

Therefore, when news broke that the same team behind *The OC* were creating a new concept, there were always going to be a lot of interested parties and actors' agents across the US were whipped up into a frenzy of anticipation. There is a rumour that *Gossip Girl* was originally pitched as a movie starring Lindsay Lohan as Blair Waldorf, but when that idea fell through, the original novels were turned into a series instead.

The auditioning process for *Gossip Girl* was brutal, with each successful actor or actress being called back at least six or seven times. Ed was no exception. Surprisingly, one rumour suggests that Ed was originally down to audition for the role of Nate Archibald (eventually taken by his future pal Chace Crawford) but his looks and super-sharp vocal delivery made the producers feel he would be better suited to play the show's bad guy, a scheming and manipulative rich kid called Chuck Bass.

Another audition rumour is that Ed initially acted in his natural English accent, but the producers felt it best that the character of Chuck was American. For many actors this would have signalled the end of their chances of success, as no amount of good acting can make up for an inaccurate accent. However, the American accent was clearly not an issue for Ed and so he kept getting called back.

The gulf between Ed's own accent and Chuck's was not the only distance between him and the character he was to play. There was also a massive distance between Chuck's privileged life and Ed's own much more modest childhood. Was it difficult to make that leap? 'We all kind of know who these people are,' he told *Company* magazine. 'I think if I was playing someone from my own background that would be more challenging. It would be hard getting in touch with yourself and things that are so everyday ... I am aware of this culture from television over the years but a lot of it came off the script for me, all credit to the writers. The way it's written it comes alive very easily ... I had my preconceived ideas of what these people should be like and it came together very organically, it felt very natural.'

The revered TV executive Les Moonves was intimately involved in the whole audition process and like his future co-stars, Ed knew that it was crucial to make the right impression on this central figure. Moonves had himself previously been an actor starring in such hits as *The Six Million Dollar Man* and *Cannon*, but it was behind the camera that he made a huge impact, as a president and CEO of numerous colossal American networks, making him one of the most powerful executives in US entertainment. Among the shows that he had previously 'green lighted' were such hits as *Friends* and *ER*. If Moonves was involved in a project, it was almost guaranteed to be a massive success, so everyone knew that the stakes were high. The final decision over who would get the part of Chuck Bass was left to former actor-turned-CBS president Les Moonves and it was Ed who got the call!

However, this did not mean that Ed could consider his career sorted; pilots often have different actors or actresses in them compared to the final series that becomes famous, so even getting this far was no guarantee of an actor's success. Even if he secured the role of Chuck Bass, there was also no guarantee as very often entire characters get written out of the eventual shows.

Media critics had flagged the forthcoming *Gossip Girl* series as a natural successor to *The OC* and it's clear from the basic ingredients that there were indeed many parallels. While the latter focussed on the relationships of the rich and famous in California's Orange County, *Gossip Girl* moved the setting 3000 miles east to the filthy rich world of Upper Manhattan. A one-bed apartment in one of this area's more prestigious blocks will cost at least $1.5 million; a large five bedroom penthouse? $10 million.

Situated between Central Park and the East River and bordered by 59th Street and 96th Street, as well as the river and Fifth Avenue on Central park, the Upper East Side is reputed to contain the greatest concentration of wealth on earth. Therefore it draws in the wealthy and super-successful form all over the world and as such, it provided the writers of *Gossip Girl* with an enviable amount of personality types to work with. Ed's character Chuck Bass is the son of a billionaire which may seem improbably but there are many such young men in this lavish area of the Big Apple.

Hollywood has used the Upper East Side many times before: among the films which feature the area are classics such as *Breakfast At Tiffany's*, *Live and Let Die*, *The*

Bonfire of the Vanities, Eyes Wide Shut and *American Psycho*.

What better place to set the pilot episode for the new series, *Gossip Girl*? The opening scene sees 'It Girl' Serena returning on a train to Manhattan and it isn't long before we are at a glitzy NY party with waiters, rich guests, huge diamonds and money everywhere. The narrator of the show is the titular anonymous blogger who creates havoc with her texts and blogs about the friendships and relationships within a group of New York socialites, including best friends Serena van der Woodsen (Blake) and Blair Waldorf (Leighton) and the rest of their circles including Dan (Penn), Nate (Chace), Jenny (Taylor Momsen), Chuck (Ed), Vanessa (Jessica), Lily (Kelly Rutherford) and Rufus (Matthew Settle).

Ed's first on-screen appearance comes, fittingly, surrounded by beautiful women, lazing on a couch at the party, smoking. The first dialogue he has is directed towards Nate Archibald, who we discover is one of his close friends. He comments on how dull life was getting when he hears Serena is heading back, while Nate is upstairs being pounced on by Blair. Ed's high-cut cheekbones and slight sneer make it clear that his character, Chuck Bass, is not short on confidence.

Gossip Girl itself has been described as 'a guilty pleasure' because many people are addicted to watching it but often deny they do so; actually it soon becomes apparent that everyone is logging on to Gossip Girl's website to keep up with the latest gossip, personal snippets, photos, rumours and so on, but few admit they do in public!

Long-time childhood friends Nate and Chuck are soon seen on a bus talking about a girl but the way that Chuck describes 'violating' her innocence immediately appalls his friend Nate, setting out early on the very different moral values of the two pals. Nate, it seems is clearly the All-American good guy; Chuck obviously isn't! From this point of view, Ed is brilliantly cast – his eyes seem to be able to narrow in a way that makes your skin crawl at the thought of what's going through his mind! Yet somehow, perhaps because of his looks, you love to hate him but find him strangely compelling at the same time. The chemistry between Nate and Chuck – established right at the show's beginning – drives many of the storylines in *Gossip Girl*. They might be chalk and cheese but their differences complement rather than contradict each other.

It doesn't take long for Chuck to move in on Serena, and the tension is palpable. He doesn't exactly play it subtly, suggesting they simply catch up, take their clothes off and stare at each other! He is the classic predatory male, he knows what he wants and he will do pretty much anything to get it. Chuck also appears to have a severely manipulative edge and his very sinister side is revealed in the kitchens of his father's restaurant when he tries to force himself on a frightened Serena. It is already very clear who the 'bad guy' in *Gossip Girl* is.

The pilot episode is mainly focused on Nate, so Chuck's role here is more to provide the dark edges, a disturbing yet completely watchable force for evil. When he and Nate are in a limo with a bunch of girls on the way to another party, you almost fear for the young girls! Easily the best line of the pilot is when Chuck says he loves 'freshmans', sounding like some deep-sea angler chasing a big catch, hungry for 'fresh meat'. When he takes an impressionable young girl called Jenny through to a back room, it really does feel like she's being thrown to the lions. As he holds Jenny's hand and the camera pans down from his dickie bow tie and thick chequered scarf to his white basketball boots, it's also clear that Chuck's style is nothing if not bold. And it is the discarded chequered scarf that leads a concerned Dan and Serena to the roof top where Chuck is apparently forcing himself on Jenny.

Serena's arrival at the party causes chaos, arguments, countless gossip-y texts being sent and Ed's character Chuck being highlighted very much as the bad guy – towering over a frightened Jenny, clearly intent on having his way, regardless of her consent. It's a sinister edge to thi show seen early on that would later cause great controversy, a furore that Ed's character would be at the very heart of. Back with the opening show however, it was a brilliant start to a series that would in a matter of days it seemed, become one of the biggest TV programmes on earth!

The pilot made the most of what became a characteristically cool soundtrack. Over the four seasons, there have been some great songs used to ramp up the atmosphere, with contributions from Rihanna, the late, great Amy Winehouse,

Albert Hammond Jr. and Angels and Airwaves. Ed would also contribute to the soundtrack, more of which later!

When the news came through that the network CW had decided to fund an entire series, it was a massive moment for Ed as well as all the other cast members. One practicality was that Ed had to relocate to New York for filming. The Brit Abroad quickly took to the 24/7 nature of life in the Big Apple. 'It's about knowing how to pick up the phone and order something!' And he has clearly taken to living in NYC and enjoying the full social benefits it offers: 'The whole buzz of the city turns me on,' he told one magazine. 'I'm a night-time kind of guy, so I love going out. I always sense potential in the night, especially during the summer. When the sun's out the girls put on nice dresses. It's like London in the summertime. There's all this energy that's been laying under the earth for eight months of the year that's just been bubbling and cooking until finally it comes out with the sun.' In fact, one of his favourite pastimes, like Chace too, is to just hang out in a bar with a few friends and shoot some pool. 'I'm a lounge guy. I love playing pool. I love finding some place where it's quiet enough that you can control the jukebox and get on with your life.'

Despite Josh Schwartz's stellar reputation, Ed openly said that the show's co-creator was not someone he had specifically targeted to work with:

'I was aware of *The OC* and it being a hit but I didn't watch it because I've never been one to sit down and watch TV shows. But now that I'm in *Gossip Girl*, I'm interested in looking at my own work and I can now see why people get drawn into storylines. From my point of view, it was great to work with someone who has a proven track record of success so they could bring that to their new project.'

Once the production team was ramping up the project to film and then broadcast the whole first season, Ed soon became very aware of the grand scale which this new show could exist on: 'I was always hopeful because we were kind of carrying on the buzz of *The OC* with the producers.'

With the full first season of *Gossip Girl* commissioned, Ed/Chuck readied himself for the opening episode, first aired on 19 September 2007. Fittingly entitled 'The Wild Brunch', the opener sees the stars of the show head for a champagne breakfast/brunch at the restaurant owned by Chuck's dad. Chuck appears seven minutes in, draped in women! He's slept with two women while Nate has crashed nearby on the couch, alone. They chat about the night before and it's clear that the two mates are somehow a perfect foil for each other.

While Blair and Serena scratch each other's eyes out, and Jenny is asking after him the morning after the night before, Chuck is too busy looking for yet more sexual conquests. Dressed in luminously bright tennis gear, Chuck confronts Dan

over the previous night's confrontation, albeit while wearing a
lime green cardigan – pure Chuck Bass style!

At the climactic brunch, while Nate, Dan and pretty much
everyone else is uncomfortable with the personal tension,
Chuck is delighted, saying it is going to be fun! He seems able
to slip effortlessly between seducing girls and threatening rival
males. It only appears to be Chuck's domineering father who
is allowed to talk down to him. Here he wears a pink striped
jacket with yellow bow tie, and a pink pin-striped shirt,
dangling the key to his suite under Blair's nose, fully knowing
that this is going to cause trouble when they bump into Serena
again. Chuck always wants to light the emotional bomb then
sit back and watch the explosion! He then revels in telling
everyone that Serena slept with her best friend's boyfriend, all
with a smirk on his face, of course. He doesn't have the last
laugh though as a fight ensues when Chuck calls Dan's
sister a slut. With the dust barely settled on the argument,
and with people's lives in tatters around him, Chuck is
exhilarated to find Serena standing alone and sees absolutely
no reason whatsoever not to make a move on her, saying he
has rooms available. You might not like his morals but you
somehow have to like his style! Chuck exits the first episode
with yet another rejection from a beautiful woman, which he
brushes off instantly without a second thought. Serena ends
the episode by binning her mobile, but it clearly won't prove
to be so easy to lose her connections with the Upper East Side
elite.

The success of *Gossip Girl* was so quick and so huge that any comparisons to *The OC* quickly seemed irrelevant. Nearly all initial reviews were excellent and more importantly a thriving and fanatical fanbase immediately took the spirit of the 'blogger' culture to heart and chatted about the show in hundreds of blogs and forums. One thing was certain: the CW network had a major hit on their hands.

Initially there had been talk of filming in Vancouver or even possibly Los Angeles, but the producers decided to plump for the real deal and instead use the same New York stages and locations as are often seen in the award-winning *Sopranos*.

However, as the show's fame accelerated in those heady first few weeks of broadcast, quiet days out filming in Manhattan became a thing of the past. Pretty soon, the security around the shoots was manic. The on-set attention of fans in New York can get very scary. 'One day when we finished shooting outside a school in New York,' Ed told *Company*, 'we had the whole school population screaming and they were ruthless and they're ten years old!'

Of course, *Gossip Girl* has its own followers but each individual actor/actress has their own set of adoring fans too. With his stunning looks, Ed has more than his fair share of admirers and on set he is often accosted by screaming and hysterical girls after a chat or a photo or autograph. They shower him with gifts such as chocolates, flowers and cakes, as well as posters and soft toys but perhaps the most unusual fan present was a lunchbox plastered in photos of both Chuck and Ed! It's not known whether Ed takes this lunchbox to use on set of *Gossip Girl* or not.

Unlike Chace Crawford however, whose character is far more 'human' (!), Ed has the benefit of Chuck often scaring some fans away. 'I see fans walking towards me,' he told the media, 'and I can see in their eyes that they're thinking, *Is he going to be nasty to me?* They seem wary, but then they get chatting and they're like, "Oh, you're nice".'

On some occasions, the fans' enthusiasm spills over and it can get genuinely scary. On one occasion, the NYPD had to be called to hold fans back after they quite literally stormed the set of *Gossip Girl* one weekend. The crew were at the glitzy Manhattan Empire Hotel filming a party scene with Ed, Blake, Penn and Taylor's characters when dozens of screaming teenage fans filled the reception. Some were trying to get to the elevator or stairwell to gain access to the rooftop so they could spy down on the filming. Shouting and screaming and much hysteria followed and hotel guests inevitably soon started to complain. After escorting the fans out into the street, they showed no signs of calming down so the police erected security barriers and placed guards on the doors to keep the fans at bay. This was only a month after similar scenes had provoked yet more complaints from local residents after dozens of Hilary Duff fans had swamped the set and local area trying to catch a glimpse of her as she filmed her guest appearance on the show.

Back on the show, Ed/Chuck's life gets more and more complex – and he gets increasingly devious! – with every episode of Season 1. With Blair dismayed at Nate's on-going feelings for Serena, she ends up in the slippery but nonetheless attractive arms of the ever-welcoming Chuck Bass (via a performance at a burlesque club!), who is more than happy to console his best friend's girl! When they eventually break up, Chuck responds like any decent Hollywood bad guy with a simple dash of blackmail! Eventually Nate and Chuck's long-standing friendship is rekindled when the bad boy of *Gossip Girl* reveals how Nate's father is still taking drugs. The two are reunited as best buddies ... after which Chuck happily goes after Blair again! Then in the finale he stands Blair up just as they are about to fly off to Tuscany together! Bad boy!

For the network to see the ratings and public response to the first season of *Gossip Girl* must have been beyond even their most optimistic predictions – the beauty of the show's central premise – the blogger – was now a marketing tool in itself as the web was covered in gossip about the show. Ed had gone from an unknown Brit actor with a few small roles under his belt in only modestly successful films to one of the hottest new faces on TV in the world. He must have felt overwhelmed by the scale and speed of the success of *Gossip Girl* ... yet at the same time, this was exactly what Ed Westwick had been working towards all his life. And there was more, much more to come ...

CHAPTER 4

The Filthy Youth

MOST ACTORS WOULD BE happy to consider a role in a smash TV show like *Gossip Girl* as quite enough to fill their lives, but for the ever-busy Ed Westwick, he had another passion which rivaled his love of acting: music. This was a long-standing affair too: after his piano lessons as a young kid had initially been overtaken by his love for football, Ed found himself listening to more and more music in his teens (like many kids do) but his fascination was more than just teenage kicks. Ed was buying music prodigiously and started to acquire an encyclopaedic knowledge of rock's history. He also started reading around the subject, dipping into Jim Morrison of the Doors' numerous books on poetry and philosophy as well as more conventional rock biographies.

As Ed headed out of his teens and pushed more and more to break through into acting as a career, he noticed that on set there was always a lot of downtime between takes. Sitting in a trailer or canteen, or even just around a filming location, Ed started to entertain himself and his co-actors with some impromptu strumming on his guitar. This soon evolved into writing songs and before long he was thinking of forming a band. Speaking in *CosmoGirl* when he was by then a famous TV star, Ed reflected on the important role music played in his life: '*Gossip Girl* feels like a regular job, it's so scheduled. Music is my release.'

In fact, the decision to form a group came a year before *Gossip Girl* had even started, when Ed clubbed together with his local mates to form a punkish band called the Filthy Youth. Alongside Ed in the line-up were band members Benjamin Lewis Allingham, Jimmy Wright, Mitch Cox and John Vooght. The Filthy Youth cited their main influences as the Rolling Stones, the Doors, Paul Weller, the Clash and modern acts such as the Strokes and the Kings of Leon. Personally, Ed will often cite an even wider array of bands as influences on him, from genuinely legendary old school acts such as the Kinks, through more modern greats such as Nirvana and also right up to more recent acts such as the Libertines.

Ed is obviously deeply immersed in his music; speaking to *CosmoGirl* he said, 'I've always connected with music. Life's not always what you see, it's what's going on in your head. Music is what comes out of your subconscious.' He's also been quoted as saying, 'Music gets inside you, music captures you. Music becomes your heartbeat. It's a drug and makes you feel whatever the song's about.'

His band is variously tagged as 'indie rock', which is generally what less-informed publications call any guitar rock that isn't U2; others have called the sound 'punk' and certainly elements of the band's image are very much in this vein, for example the spray-painted logo, which is not dissimilar to the graffiti-style of street artists such as Banksy. It's worth noting that the band themselves tag their genre as 'Indie/Punk/Rock'.

The Filthy Youth's early gigs were almost exclusively in and around the English capital of London. One review of a gig at the 'Indiesexual' club in the southern English county in April 2007 described them as 'everything you expect from a rock and roll band' including a charismatic frontman, and said some of their tunes were 'blinding'. Another notable gig was at a pub called The Courts in the sleepy southern English county of Dorset, which also received very favourable local press. More positive reviews followed: 'Great Band, fantastic live piece,' said *The Man Who Could*'s reviewer, also in 2007. 'This bunch are going places, the lyrics are delivered with style and character, the punky yet catchy riffs are original. Keep your eyes out, these boys are ready to roll, the live act is tremendous with a great and riotous fan base screaming "Filthy Filthy Youth!" They will surely be a band to stick in your mind.'

The press reaction to the band was always going to be skewed later on due to Ed's super-fame, but before he was even on *Gossip Girl* there was a definite interest just because of their sound, such as this review from musicandfestivals.com:

'Looking for our first band to review in unsigned finds went far too smoothly as I simply selected "genre indie" on MySpace and took a pot luck shot on the first page of results. Hey presto, The Filthy Youth! This is my kind of band with storytelling lyrics and a sound that gives an acknowledging nod to many others while still remaining different. [All the] tracks on their MySpace page demand playing to the end. I can't help think there is a hint of [Pete] Doherty in there, especially as the frontman sounds like him, but that's not a bad thing!'

The Doherty link to Ed was a popular comparison, with some reviews saying they were clearly heavily influenced by that man's band, the Libertines. 'The sunny guitar riffs, witty shouts and stumbling, dry vocals on tracks like "Orange" and "Pirate", surely wouldn't be out of place on [a Libertines album],' wrote theregoesthefear.com. 'Although the Doherty imitation can get a bit clichéd after a while, the Filthy Youth still bang out undeniably decent tunes and there certainly is a gap in the market right now for an indie-punk band such as this trendy five … the Filthy Youth are still an undeniably good band.'

Despite these positive reviews, the Filthy Youth made little impact initially, but as soon as their lead singer Ed was appearing on *Gossip Girl*, focus on the band inevitably heated up, so that they quickly attracted far more press and public attention. For his more die-hard fans, it was hard not to make the connection with his lead singer role in the Filthy Youth and Ed's appearance on *Casualty* all those years ago as Johnny Cullin, the frustrated frontman who argues with his guitarist even as the stage is falling down around (and onto!) them.

Extra publicity for the band was obviously a huge upside to Ed's *Gossip Girl* role but in Season 1 he was able to ramp this help up even more, when two of the band's songs were used during an episode. This was a massive coup for an unsigned British band. The episode was called 'School Lies' and the songs in question were 'Come Flash All You Ladies' and 'Orange'. Ed co-wrote and sang lead vocals on both tracks.

The first of these tunes starts with a clanging guitar intro, jarring in a very retro fashion akin to the Strokes. This is cleverly mixed in with a semi-reggae rhythm that chugs along as Ed's vocals pile in, all characterful and heavily accented. There's an intricate drum-rolling backdrop to the chorus lead-in too, and altogether the song really asks for your attention. Vocally Ed sounds like the front man of the Kooks with a hint of Iggy Pop or the MC5, a clear sign that he knows his music history. The mid-section of the song features a reverbed middle-eight which suggests just how much they like the Doors. It's a garage rock sound that owes more to the early punk pioneers of the late 1960s such as the Stooges than it does to the more recent 'indie rock' bands that are often rather wrongly associated with the band. Played behind the on-screen luxury of *Gossip Girl* it's easy to see why this made a very energetic, fierce and effective soundtrack.

Ed has made it clear that this song is about certain types of women he has met throughout his life! Rather cheekily, given the song's title, when you visit the band's MySpace page you are invited to submit your own 'filthy youth pictures'! (nearly 1,000 'filthy youths' have obliged). I suspect there have been quite a few pictures submitted that the band was not able to leave up on their site!

The second featured song 'Orange' opens with a carefully picked guitar over a thumping backbeat, with Ed's vocals quickly piling in with a late 1970s Two Tone authenticity. Again there's a clear reggae influence to the guitar work and the tumbling drums and simple yet effective bass lines make this a very upbeat number. Ed's opening 'Allo!' is pure London boy, no doubt quite a surprise to those *Gossip Girl* fans who were yet to realise he isn't American. Ed is on record as saying this song is about being out on the town with your mates and 'ripping it up'.

The episode these songs feature in sees the group of friends break into the school swimming pool but their larking about almost ends in tragedy when one of them nearly drowns. This near-miss appalls the school authorities who vow to expel whoever is responsible. Fittingly, the episode sees Chuck at his evil best, as he tries to get Vanessa to help him blackmail Blair! And all the time he's soundtracking his own dark deeds!

Other tracks by the band have the same garage rock feel, clanging guitars, very agitated and energetic drums, edgy vocals which skip between spoken word and very likeable singing, with an overwhelming sense that this is a band full of energy. Listening to the Filthy Youth without knowing who was the lead singer would definitely make you want to see the band live. (For his part, Ed's favourite Filthy Youth track is 'Le Soleil'.)

Even with his role as Chuck Bass generating such success and attention, Ed was still in love with his music. Citing Jim Morrison again he said, 'It wasn't just about the music, it was a show. On stage I'm a showman. I wouldn't say I'm a rock star though ... all right, in my own world I am!' However, with Ed's profile sky high, there was a fear expressed – even by his own PR team – that 'overexposure' was a risk: this is an easy trap to fall into when a career is going stellar and can eventually lead to disinterest from a previously fascinated public. There were risks for the band too – to date they have not signed a record deal even though their MySpace and web profile is very healthy. To this extent, there is a possibility that Ed's TV fame was sometimes more of a curse than a blessing, as the material they were writing was genuinely talented but many record companies may have steered clear of the act because of worries about the 'credibility' of an apparent 'pretty boy' TV star playing rock and roll.

When talking to MTV News, Ed's bandmate Jimmy Wright seemed very philosophical about the positive effects of his singer's acting fame:

'It's great to get involved in *Gossip Girl*, crossing over both mediums … It's very different out [in America] as we have gained a younger audience due to *Gossip Girl*, which is great. But we formed the band before there even was a *Gossip Girl* so perhaps that's why we have an older audience at home. [And when] two of our songs were on one of the episodes, [it] gained us more fans, who perhaps before had never had the chance to listen to us.' One of their subsequent Stateside shows from 2008 at the The Annnex in New York – when Ed was already a fully fledged *Gossip Girl* star – was captured in a drawing by Todd DiCiurcio that features on the band's MySpace page.

Perhaps inevitably with his *Gossip Girl* success, the Filthy Youth became an increasingly impossible passion for Ed. First of all the practicalities of living in New York and his crazy schedule would make it hard to even rehearse, never mind go on tour (the rest of the band are based in the UK). And even if for some reason he was to suddenly have a few weeks completely free (unlikely!) the chances of the band playing the modest venues they inhabited and not being swamped by thousands of *Gossip Girl* fans were pretty small! This would then force his band to play bigger and bigger venues just to accommodate the *Gossip Girl* fan base which in itself would make the 'intimate' experience a contradiction in terms. Ed loves the rock and roll side of the band, the personal venues, the edgy feel, all of which would probably be lost if he was playing to an arena full of *Gossip Girl* fans. Regardless of all this, the simple reality is that he is super-busy in New York, 3,000 miles away; the Filthy Youth's future, at least with Ed Westwick on vocals, was always going to be tricky.

Delving further, you can get an indication of the level of Ed's influence on the band's profile by zooming into the number of plays that their songs have had – two and a half million! Interestingly though, you would expect the two songs featured in *Gossip Girl* to have been listened to the most, but it is in fact 'Boys Don't Smoke' (the first song offered) that dwarfs all the other tunes, with close to a million plays. Notably, at the time of writing, Ed is listed as their first 'Friend' alongside over 40,000 others! (For fans of Ed less interested in the band, he's listed as their 'Top Friend'; clicking through to his link takes you to a MySpace page coded simply '125291160' next to a picture of Ed in a crisp white shirt.)

Clicking through to the Filthy Youth's MySpace photos – let's face it, most *Gossip Girl* fans will be doing that pretty quickly! – there is a satisfyingly large number of shots of Ed. Stepping back from the TV celebrity he boasts for a moment, the photos look every bit the cool rock star, very much in the vein of a Liam Gallagher of Oasis or Richard Ashcroft of the Verve. In all the shots it is clear the venues are small, intimate and probably suffering from the sticky beer-covered floors of all good music 'toilets', in sharp contrast to the ultra-glamour of *Gossip Girl*. Behind him on one pub wall are the words 'I Bet I Give Up Gambling', hardly the gloss of an Upper East

Side lifestyle but perhaps just as seedy. Perhaps not surprisingly, the photo with the most views is the shot of him shirtless! Notably, the photos of the other band members have typically around 2,000 views, whereas Ed's have in the region of 25,000+ each. The tagged photos are mainly fans posting, with the requisite 'I'm a filthy youth' caption; there's even a picture of a baby in a vest emblazoned with that legend! In the comments, my own favourite is the cheeky little remark from one 'Friend' which says, tongue firmly planted in cheek, 'We should make music together!'

Live clips of the band reveal Ed to be far more chaotic and wild onstage than he sounds on record! One particular clip sees him singing with a glass of (what appears to be) spirits and a cigarette in his hand, clearly keen to have a good time; another clip sees him holding *two* glasses of beer and a cigarette!

In 2009 the inevitable happened and Ed came to the conclusion he needed to leave the Filthy Youth:

'I found it difficult to juggle music with my filming commitments,' was his understandable reasoning. Explaining himself more on UK TV he said, 'I was in a band once upon a time. I was singing. It was a good time. I just found myself being so busy tied up with the show and everything like that. Music, I absolutely adore, as I'm sure we all do. It was something that I really enjoyed but it was just so difficult to have time to do these things.'

The reality is that with *Gossip Girl* being such a huge success, it may well be that Ed's music career has to take a (possibly permanent) back seat. There are precedents where TV stars have made a success of their bands – most obviously Jared Leto of Thirty Seconds to Mars and to a lesser degree Johnny Depp – but these are the exception.

That said, maybe Ed could take a leaf out of Taylor Momsen's music book! His co-star in *Gossip Girl* – she plays Jenny Humphrey – has enjoyed a considerable degree of success with her parallel rock music career in the band the Pretty Reckless. Taylor is on record as saying that although she loves her 'day job', music is more personal and is something she lives for. This echoes Ed's comments that music comes from your own subconscious rather than a script. Unlike the Filthy Youth, Taylor's band signed to one of the biggest record companies in the world, Interscope; Taylor is also the songwriter, singer and even plays some guitar. The Pretty Reckless are a full-on touring band too, and have supported the Veronicas in a 2009 jaunt across America. Their debut album *Light Me Up* fared well on the charts as did a batch of singles. Although cynics will always frown upon such a joint career, Taylor does seem to have had more success than the Filthy Youth to date.

As if that wasn't enough musicality for one show, Leighton Meester – Chuck's on-off love interest in *Gossip Girl* – has also launched a music career. At the time of writing, she is working on a debut album that she told MTV was 'a good mixture of hip-hop-sounding, very vibe-y music'. She'd previously recorded the song 'Inside the Black' for the teenage horror film *Drive Thru* in 2007 (which also featured Penn Badgley) so she had previous form, but notably her marketing team felt it was a sideline to her acting career that they wanted to treat with caution and were turning down interviews specifically about the music project for some time. Her 2009 debut single featuring Robin Thicke was followed the year after by 'Your Love's a Drug'. Again her fascination with music and the very different artistic outlet it provides mirrored what her *Gossip Girl* co-stars had previously said: 'I've always done [music]. It's so cool because it's a completely different creative process.'

Looking at the acting career of Ed, his rise to fame has been somewhat meteoric – although he had been in films and TV shows previously, the speed of *Gossip Girl*'s success catapulted him to global fame almost overnight. Consequently any non-acting ambitions he may have had, such as being in a band, have necessarily taken a back seat. Whether he will come back to his music career is unclear, and indeed the chances of him being given a fair crack of the whip in terms of earning critics' respect are probably quite slim. Take this headline from MTV: 'You know you love them … but will you buy albums from Blair and Chuck?' This is probably part of the problem: those actors' lives are now so intertwined with those of their characters – rightly or wrongly – in the eyes of the watching public that to carve out a credible music career might just be impossible. Still, never discount Ed rocking up onstage any time soon; he has mentioned the idea of starting a new band in New York and clearly still craves involvement in music: 'I'm sure, you haven't heard the last of me yet.'

CHAPTER 5

Movie Mania

THE YEAR AFTER ED made his *Gossip Girl* debut, he starred in another big screen role, playing Lawrence Carter in the low budget indie comedy-drama *Son of Rambow*. In film terms, it is essentially a 'coming of age' movie about two schoolboys' rites of passage and friendship. The production team known as Hammer & Tongs were behind this film – a lofty duo indeed, comprising of Garth Jennings and Nick Goldsmith, who had been developing the movie for several years only to have to put it on hold when they were asked to make *The Hitchhiker's Guide to the Galaxy* no less. For Ed to get a role in their second feature film was another big coup for the *Gossip Girl* actor.

In contrast to *Gossip Girl*'s environment, this film is set very much in the English comprehensive school system of the 1980s, where the two key characters – Will and Lee (played by Bill Milner and Will Poulter respectively) – first meet. Will is a sheltered boy whose family's involvement in a puritanical religious group called The Brethren means he must not watch TV or films and even has to leave the classroom if the teacher shows a documentary. On one such class exit, he bumps into the school's delinquent, Lee, and they strike up an unlikely friendship. Ed plays Lee's bullying older brother and surrogate father figure Lawrence who is keen to get into making movies; Lee 'borrows' Lawrence's filming equipment and with the help of a bemused but increasingly excited Will, they set about making a film together. They choose to make a spin-off of *Rambo* because this is the first film that the sheltered boy ever sees. The film follows their ambitious amateur film production and plots their growing friendship along the way, as well as Will's mother's realisation that she has to let her young son find his own way in life.

The starring roles were played brilliantly by the young pairing of Bill Milner and Will Poulter. Alongside them were Jessica Stevenson as Will's mother, struggling to keep her son away from the modern world she is so fearful of, as well as Adam Godley as the Brethren's leader. There is even a delightful cameo appearance by comedy legend Eric Sykes, who plays the old man who is supposedly Rambo. Ed's character is not one of the major roles nor is he particularly likeable but when he is on screen, he acts with some prowess. Unfortunately on the film's official trailer, he doesn't feature at all.

Of course, the English comprehensive school system in which the film is set is something that Ed is perfectly familiar with, having been through exactly such a schooling in Stevenage himself. In fact, filming was almost entirely done at Berkhamsted, a town only forty minutes west of where Ed was brought up, so he had the added bonus of being able to stay with his parents while filming! The film is peppered with 1980s pop-culture references although Ed would have been too young to experience the large mobile phones and over-the-top haircuts! His character Lawrence has a fairly awful 1980s fashion sense, including an array of vile polo-neck sweaters, some too-tight slacks and even a rather dodgy dressing gown! Mind you, Ed's mean and moody character does drive a TVR7, the classic British sports car, so he's got some taste. And although Lawrence is an arrogant and overbearing character, he's certainly not as manipulative as Chuck Bass!

The film was initially shown at the Sundance Film Festival where there was something of an industry buzz surrounding the project and a heated bidding war to secure its rights (eventually going for the biggest sum of all the available movies at the festival). The film was released to the public in May 2008 and was immediately met with warm reviews. The critics were impressed and almost all of them gave the film a positive reception which could only be a big plus for Ed's acting career. Filmjabber.com said it was, 'Filmed in a creatively madcap, home-made style with a mostly amateur cast and a wry, comic-tinged nostalgia, creative visionaries Garth Jennings and Nick Goldsmith manage to capture both the agony and the giddy ecstasy of a camcorder childhood with humor, poignancy and a rousing dose of cinematic panache.' The often hard-to-please *Empire* magazine agreed, saying 'a potentially disposable, tongue-in-cheek *First Blood* piss-take turns out to be a deeply effective, surprisingly touching tale of family and childhood friendship.'

In fact, the movie appeared in the 'Top Ten of the Year' lists of many notable film critics, so this was a very credible and successful next step for Ed to have been involved in. And his own reviews were very good too, with sugarscape.com even going so far as to say 'we reckon he is the new Joaquin Phoenix!'

Aside from critics, there was one other famous fan of the movie – Sylvester Stallone himself! The obvious reference to his war veteran character Rambo in the title meant that he would need to approve of the project ... which he did completely. This was high praise indeed. With takings exceeding $10 million and such positive reviews, Ed had successfully made another step up the film career ladder.

Back at *Gossip Girl* Central, there were no such worries about mediocre reviews or limited commercial appeal. Season 2 had been a huge ratings smash and during this time we saw Chuck's character develop in very interesting – and sometimes disturbing! – ways.

Season 2 is set in the Senior Year of the main characters' lives and Chuck is just as manipulative as ever! This series of episodes really highlights Chuck and Nate's friendship and in turn this made both Ed and Chace Crawford probably the biggest stars of the show worldwide. We also see Chuck's on-going inability to commit to any serious relationship, even though his feelings for Blair seem deep and genuine. Most obviously, this season was a shocking one for Chuck as his cold-hearted billionaire father dies in a car crash and thereafter his character seems somewhat at sea, not least after we discover that Chuck's mother died in childbirth and his father never forgave his son for that loss. The season finale shows Chuck and Blair sharing a much-anticipated kiss as they finally start a relationship, so there were clearly no signs of Ed's prominence in the show dwindling.

A simple web search for 'Gossip Girl' will throw up thousands of sites and mentions, all reflecting the fact that the fans of the show were on-line 24/7, chatting, discussing and second-guessing the show's next move. And Chuck was always at the centre of any discussions, people couldn't believe what he got up to! In the aftermath of *Gossip Girl*'s second season, Ed's life was changed forever.

The most obvious reflection of the show's success was the huge number of fans who were still turning up at any filming on the streets of Manhattan. The cast were always bombarded with gifts and very often the screams of fans would mean retakes. A second aspect of the huge success of *Gossip Girl* and its impact on Ed's life is the massive volume of magazine, TV and radio interviews he has to do. At times, this can be exhausting but, along with Chace Crawford, Ed is one of the show's best promoters. Just like Chace, almost every interview he faced asks him if he is single, who the hottest girl on set is and what's his dream date, his favourite look in a girl, his chat-up lines etc.

Like Chace, Ed's profile is such that he also has many YouTube and related clips online; indeed, several fans have compiled their own montages of clips often featuring both the actors together, so for example you have one such snip called 'Private pictures of Chace and Ed'.

Just how big the show had become was reflected in *New York* magazine when that prestigious publication ran a cover feature on *Gossip Girl* with the tag line, 'Best Show Ever'. And, just like Chace, again Ed was considered so famous that by 2009 he was invited to attend The White House Correspondents' Dinner – a celebrity-drenched occasion that on that night also saw such famous faces as Ben Affleck, Eva Longoria and John Cusack among the 2000 or so guests.

Although Ed had enjoyed a small degree of success before *Gossip Girl*, this level of fame was on an entirely new level. He was clearly having a blast, as he told *Company* magazine: 'The whole project was absolute fun, you know whether it was wearing great clothes or driving around Manhattan in limousines. The whole thing was a whirlwind. Pretty crazy for a 20-year-old.'

CHAPTER 6

A Sideways Step

NEXT UP FOR ED in his film career was a distinct change of direction away from the endearing comedy and feel-good factor of *Son of Rambow*. Taking a very definite sharp turn, he signed up next for the supernatural thriller *100 Feet*, which was to be written and directed by Eric Red. Eric is an American screenwriter and director who had previously penned highly acclaimed horror flicks such as *The Hitcher*, *Near Dark* and *Bad Moon*. The former is considered by many in the genre to be one of the finest horror cult films of all time. Eric himself described his new film *100 Feet* as 'a classical-style contemporary ghost story that focuses on suspense and terror, not gore. It is old school in that it is character- and story-driven and you care a lot about the people in it.'

Alongside Ed in the intriguing cast was Famke Janssen, a beautiful Dutch actress who had enjoyed some high profile roles in various *Star Trek* TV shows and the *X-Men* series as well as *Nip/Tuck*. She had garnered some acclaim for numerous film roles in movies such as *Goldeneye* and *Fathers*

& *Sons* and in 2003 had even won the 'International Star of the Year' award. So once again Ed was putting himself in the same milieu as some very serious actors and actresses.

The film was a very dark and at times harrowing account of Marnie, a woman who has killed her abusive policeman husband after years of him beating her. She is released early from her manslaughter prison sentence only to be cast under house arrest in Brooklyn in a home still spattered with blood and where her husband's ghost soon begins to haunt and then attack her. The '100 feet' of the title refers to the distance Marnie is allowed to go from a detector set in her hallway before an alarm goes off, alerting the police.

The entire cinematic feel of the movie is very frightening and broody, a far cry indeed from the gloss and glamour of Ed's day job at *Gossip Girl*. The exterior shots were filmed on location in NYC so this was something Ed was perfectly used to doing of course; the interior shots were filmed on a studio set which gave him a great chance to flex his acting muscles. But the heart of the movie was the Big Apple: 'New York City cannot be faked shooting anywhere else, like Canada,' Eric Red has said, echoing the sentiments of the *Gossip Girl* producers. 'You have to film in New York.' The house where the film is set is a so-called 'brownstone' home, older, darker and more foreboding than the more swanky loft apartment that Ed was used to living in!

Ed plays Joey, an attractive 18-year-old delivery boy with a small-time criminal background who delivers groceries to the

Ed's guitar is his constant companion, whether playing with his band
The Filthy Youth or strumming away on set.

Ed is a huge football fan, and no mean player on the pitch himself!

Opposite: Chuck Bass has single-handedly made the 'preppy' look high fashion once again.

Chuck and Blair share a passionate kiss on the set of *Gossip Girl*.

Opposite: Ed with his ex-girlfriend and fellow *Gossip Girl* star, Jessica Szohr.

Opposite: Ed's striking fashion sense and role as Chuck Bass scooped him the *GQ* 'Breakthrough Talent of the Year' award in 2010.

Ed is now a regular at catwalk shows and fashion launches around the world.

The boy from Stevenage meets his fans in London.

main character Marnie. At first Ed is simply delivering groceries but he soon strikes up a friendship with Marnie after she pleads with him to visit her every day; sadly this proves to be his death warrant. On one occasion, they have sex – while her dead husband's spirit watches suspended on the ceiling – and after this, events spiral until Joey's fate is sealed. Eventually Marnie's husband violently assaults Joey, breaking his bones and agonisingly torturing him, before finally snapping his neck. When Ed/Joey's body is found, Marnie is then charged with his murder.

The suspense in the story was fuelled by using long takes where the audience is literally on the edge of their seats and this visual style is then jarred by quick cuts when the horror sequences crash in. It's a compelling mix to watch and Ed's smooth handsome features and convincing character acting sit well in the twisted tale.

Speaking to the media in the wake of the film's release, Eric Red was very positive about Ed's acting and professionalism: 'He's a young Englishman who plays a believable Brooklyn kid, accent and all ... Ed was offbeat, against-the-grain casting. He is a realistic-looking and -sounding kid, not one of these interchangeable generic television pretty kids you see all the time.' High praise indeed.

Although the plot was an intriguing and clever twist on a conventional horror tale, the movie received very tepid responses and in fact went straight to TV, debuting on the Syfy channel in April 2009. The following week saw the DVD released too, so this was not a huge box office smash as Ed perhaps would have liked.

Unfortunately, Ed's next film was also destined not to trouble the upper reaches of the movie charts. The initial signs had been good however: *S Darko – A Donnie Darko Tale* was a sequel to the well-received cult hit *Donnie Darko* from 2001. That original movie centred around a troubled teenager plagued by visions and undergoing psychiatric treatment, in a film that mashes up suspense, time-travel and a dash of surreal action! The first film had starred Drew Barrymore, Patrick Swayze and Jake Gyllenhaal and although it had been a low-budget production which received only very modest reviews and small box office takings on its initial release, it went on to gain much critical acclaim and cult status. Notably the original film was shot entirely within 28 days – the time in the movie which the central character Donnie has left before the end of the world. The film was originally going straight to DVD but then it gained a general release through Drew Barrymore's production company.

The Chris Fisher-directed sequel in which Ed stars is set seven years later and centres around Donnie's younger sister Sam, played by Daveigh Chase (who had also played that character in the original film). Starting the movie as a professional dance hopeful, Sam's life seems far more sedate than the bizarre world of her brother, but soon she too begins to suffer similarly odd and frightening dreams and sporadic sleepwalking episodes, just as her brother had in the first film.

Ed appears very early on in the movie, when Sam's car breaks down and his character – another 'bad boy' called Randy! – escorts them to a local motel. His character has been described as 'a small-town guy who never really lived up to his potential'. The film then spirals into a quite weird tale of time-travel, wormholes and meteorites!

The new movie was shot in Utah, a very different location to Manhattan for Ed but he enjoyed the change of surroundings. He was also excited to be in a sequel of a movie that he'd loved, despite its flaws: 'I probably saw [the first film] two or three years ago,' he told *Interview* magazine's David Colman in 2009. 'I think it was a boring night, and we rented a movie. Obviously I'd heard a lot about it . . . This was before *Gossip Girl*. When I first saw it I didn't really get all the hype. Then, of course, you look closer. Richard Kelly did a great job, and so did the cast.'

Sadly, the new film received some scathing reviews. Writing in Filmcritic.com, Bill Gibron said: '*S Darko* couldn't be more tedious. It takes everything that Kelly invested in his original and reduces it down to a thick, viscous sludge of clichés, stereotypes, and poorly written dialogue.' However, the *San Francisco Examiner* had some praise for Ed and said 'the supporting cast, featuring Ed Westwick and the always reliable John Hawkes is solid. But this *Donnie Darko* tale is all style, no substance – a superficial imitation that retraces the original's twists and turns but offers none of its own.' Unfortunately the unpopular sequel suffered the fate of going straight to DVD (that its predecessor had narrowly avoided) and was seen by many critics as a cash-in on a much better original. The most interest that the film seemed to generate were the behind-the-scenes photos of Ed with blood all over his face and head, for scenes in which his character Randy is seriously injured. Still, despite the disappointing reception, Ed was still seeing positives: 'It was great to not only be around different actors and crew after ... *Gossip Girl*, but to be involved in something that's got that connection to such a cult hit.' Unfortunately, it seems that the very 'cult' nature of the original meant that most people were predisposed to disliking the sequel, and perhaps the legacy of the original just proved too much to live with.

CHAPTER 7

His New BFF!

FORTUNATELY, ALTHOUGH ED'S MOVIE career was stumbling at times, *Gossip Girl* was just going from strength to strength. In the endless hours and hours of PR and interviews that Ed did for the show, it was interesting to note that he was usually paired up with his best friend on the set – Chace Crawford, who plays Nate Archibald. It's interesting to note that (just as with this book) Ed and Chace are very often presented as some kind of *Gossip Girl* 'dream team'. In those promotional interviews there seemed to be a genuine chemistry between the two, with Chace regularly making Ed snigger at his silly jokes. They were quite the comedy duo during interviews and many a cheeky side glance or saucy comment was made between the friends. Cheekily, when Ed was once asked who he would like to play him in a movie about his life, he said Chace Crawford! (As well as Daniel Day-Lewis though!)

They often went to gigs taking in such bands as the Arctic Monkeys and would regularly be photographed at restaurants or bars in the city. The two had bonded quickly on set and so it was not entirely surprising that they decided to rent an apartment together! When this news broke, the idea of two of American TV's biggest heart-throbs flat-sharing sent *Gossip Girl* fan sites into a frenzy!

The reality was that they had made the decision for practical reasons as much as anything else: 'He's my good buddy,' Chace told MediaBlvd.com. 'And, it cut the cost. We got a really nice place. Otherwise, we'd be hung up.' They also weren't sure if *Gossip Girl* would last so the expense of committing to a tenancy on their own was something they both wanted to avoid. Of course, such practicalities seem absurd now that they are both so famous but back then it was a very real financial consideration they had to think about. With a relocation fee of $7,000 towards their costs, both actors were potentially looking at forking out large sums of money just to get a place to live.

They both laughed at the intense interest in their living arrangements such as their household habits, who left out-of-date food in the fridge and so on. They both also denied rumours that there were rather a lot of crazy parties up there although the apartment was no doubt a true bachelor's pad! Ed's love of music started to rub off on Chace as the Brit introduced the All-American boy to a number of classic English bands such as Oasis, Stereophonics and the Kooks. And of course Ed's guitar was always close to hand. '[Now] I'm not in a band, I'm just a brilliant solo artist ... I've got this fantastic guitar I bought not long ago which is a 1957 Les Paul

Junior, I've got this tube amp from 1952 as well, so I annoy my neighbours in my apartment building by blaring music out at four o'clock in the morning!'

Rumours also circulated that Westwick and Crawford were especially messy but this was something that they strongly denied, saying this had come from people who'd not even set foot in their flat. They had a housekeeper who kept on top of things for them and Chace has since said they, 'ran a good ship there for a while.' (Notably, when Ed is not filming *Gossip Girl* and does not need to be in America for work, he will usually fly home to see his family and he stays with them at his childhood Stevenage home. This proves that despite all the fame and money and success, he is still a very grounded and decent person.)

Ed enjoyed introducing the All-American boy Chace to numerous English phrases such as saying 'rubbish' for garbage and 'garage' too and occasionally in interviews, Chace could almost be heard to have a tiny hint of an English accent! Funnily enough, the two hadn't hung out much during the filming of the pilot because Ed's girlfriend of the time was staying over with him. But as soon as the main series started, they became pals and roomed together, and things changed: 'We went for it. You kind of become brothers in that sense. And we're going through a similar craziness of the show. We don't have the same hours – it's not like we have the same 9-to-5 job every day and work in the same cubicle! It's very lop-sided in fact. It's a good situation and it's worked out well.'

Inevitably and perhaps farcically too, their close friendship led to entirely incorrect rumours that they were in fact having a sexual relationship – something which they both obviously strenuously denied but which still made them laugh with bewilderment. *Gossip Girl* has a very large gay following, which *Out* magazine called 'a cultural phenomenon whose early adopters weren't actually teenage girls but rather gay men trapped in arrested development or seeking to vicariously prolong their youth.'

Due to their fame and exceptional good looks, Ed and Chace had strong gay followings too and both had been featured in numerous gay and lesbian publications. In the novels of *Gossip Girl*, Chuck Bass is even eventually revealed to be bisexual. And their living together in their New York apartment was also commented on. Ed was quick to point out just how ridiculous these rumours were: 'I just laugh them off,' he was quoted as saying by www.contactmusic.com. 'What are you going to do? People who know me and Chace and the cast know that we are all great friends. And that's the extent of it all. Those things that go around are just amusing to us, really.'

In an massive cover feature for *Rolling Stone* which featured many of the stars of *Gossip Girl*, Ed further denied any sexual relationship with Chace: '[The rumours are] f**king ridiculous! It's funny because I love this f**king dude dearly. I would die for this f**king dude. He's my brother. But, by God, we are so into our women it's ridiculous. But what are you going to do about it? Get pissed off and stay home and cry about it?'

Perhaps inevitably, fans of *Gossip Girl* eventually found out the exact address of the apartment that the two co-stars shared and once that had happened, things started to get a little weird! Love letters started dropping on to their mat each day by the dozen. 'I've been getting some weird mail, that's for sure,' Ed revealed in contactmusic.com. 'There have been a couple of nights where some of the girls ... have obviously got a bit drunk and written love letters and slipped them under the door. We have one stuck up on the fridge ... She goes on some rant about how she is not like other girls and I should give her a call and we should hang out.'

In 2009, the two pals decided it was finally time to get their own places. 'Frat time's over,' Chace told *People*, 'I needed my own space.' Ed stayed put while Chace moved out to the financial district but the two remain the best of friends.

Meanwhile in *Gossip Girl*'s Season 3, Chuck and Nate are still great pals too, despite all the on-off relationships with Blair and Serena! Chuck and Blair are in love and seem happy and soon have to team up in business to fight off the malicious attacks of his (possibly even more evil!) uncle. It must be in the family – but just as Chuck seems content with Blair, he offers her up as a 'bribe' to his uncle Jack in exchange for keeping a hotel he had invested in. Nice! Unsurprisingly, Blair doesn't take this too well, and they break up again. When he tries to reconcile with her at the top of the Empire State Building, her lateness is mistaken for indifference and he is distraught – yet more signs that Chuck is human after all and ... whisper it ... even likeable. They make up, then they break up again, etc., but when he flies to Prague to clear his head, Chuck fans were horrified to see him shot in the stomach by muggers. The season ends with Ed's character lying in an alleyway, possibly dead. For Ed fans around the world, it was a shocking climax to a brilliant 'Chuck' season.

CHAPTER 8

On The Couch …
In The Spotlight

A WAY FROM *GOSSIP GIRL*, next up for Ed was a road trip as he had to travel to LA to work on an episode in the third season of the hit TV show *Californication*, featuring *X Files* star David Duchovny. The show's lead is a troubled novelist who is struggling with writer's block, constantly living to excess in numerous ways (!) and barely managing to maintain his relationship with his long-time girlfriend, all the time while teaching creative writing to a class of teenagers. It was an award-winning show for Showtime TV and had scooped an Emmy and a Golden Globe, so it was a great notch in Ed's career CV. The main criticism of the show is directed at the often very explicit nature of the stories and scenes, with one episode seeing a nun give Duchovny's character oral sex!

In a neat nod to the hugely successful *Twilight* series featuring the likes of Robert Pattinson – which *Gossip Girl* and Chace and Ed had been compared to recently as a massive teen phenomena – Ed plays a student by the name of Chris 'Balt' Smith who becomes fascinated with vampire literature in an episode called 'The Land of Rape and Honey'.

Ed's character is one of the very first on-screen, sitting in his teacher Duchovny's class reading aloud a short story he has written about vampires. Ed/Balt is dressed in a cardigan and slacks, with a check shirt ironed neatly. Although the story is very old-fashioned, Ed's character seems completely engrossed in his own words, even though his teacher is so unimpressed and bored that he is texting his daughter. Matters get worse for Balt when his classmates, including one of his best friends, ridicule his attempts at creative writing.

There is an undercurrent that Ed/Balt is homosexual and has designs on Duchovny's teacher character, and this suspicion is confirmed after class when Balt reveals he has a crush on his teacher. Taken aback, Duchovny's character brushes this approach aside awkwardly then tries to give his eager pupil a reality check about his mundane vampire writing – he tells Ed's character that, 'The world doesn't need any more lame vampire fiction', a clear reference to *Twilight*. He even compares the pupil's writing to toilet paper.

Distraught by the rejection, Balt/Ed overdoses and ends up in a hospital bed, nursed by his buxom roommate Jackie. Horrified that his 'reality check' chat might have caused the overdose, Duchovny's character goes to visit Ed/Balt in hospital and clumsily tries to make him feel better by embarrassingly revealing details of his own teenage gay experiences, before apologising for berating Ed/Balt's fledgling fiction.

Speaking about the show, Ed said quite accurately that, 'It's one of those shows that you'd probably struggle to watch with your mother or father, you'd probably die of embarrassment!' Ed's performance was only a guest slot but it garnered good reviews nonetheless, with *NYMag.com* saying 'Westwick is really pretty great here'.

It's nothing new for the real lives of TV stars to be confused with the characters they play on screen by certain members of the public and their fans. Generations of soap actors are used to being called their on-screen name in the street. Usually this is simply a part of their job, but sometimes it can be more sinister than that. British actor Danny Miller brilliantly played a homosexual character in the soap *Emmerdale* but was attacked on a night out by two men whose motive was alleged to be because of Miller's gay character. Bizarrely this was only two weeks after Miller had reported receiving hate mail because he'd revealed he was actually heterosexual in real life.

One big problem for Ed – and the rest of the *Gossip Girl* cast of course – is that with most of them living and being seen working on the streets of the Big Apple, it's hard for many fans to keep a clear definition between real life and fiction. Of course, it doesn't help matters when members of the cast date each other! Clearly Chuck fans would want Ed to date Blair, sorry, Leighton Meester, but in fact the romance that was brewing on set headed in the direction of Vanessa Abrams, played by the stunning Jessica Szohr. Jessica was born in Wisconsin and although her real-life beauty was very striking, her character in the show was rather more down-to-earth, the likeable Vanessa being one of the few kids of *Gossip Girl* who seems a little more in touch with reality! She had won the role in a rather unusual audition – the story goes that Jessica had been at a Labor Day barbecue and was chatting to a few people and having a great time, oblivious to the fact that one of the faces she'd been enjoying some food with was an executive producer of *Gossip Girl* – he'd immediately contacted her manager and asked her to audition for the show!

In late 2008, rumours had started circulating that Jessica and Ed were an item, or at the very least close friends and there was not a great deal of denial coming from either camp! *Gossip Girl* blogs and forums went crazy with people discussing whether this was all true and the Internet began to feature personal snaps of the two apparently out on dates around Manhattan. Once the more mainstream press got hold of the story it was inevitably going to be a big splash. In November 2008 they were spotted apparently 'smooching' at Dallas airport and soon after *US Weekly* reported they had 'locked lips' at the New York Knicks–Los Angeles Lakers Game in New York, with Ed 'often whispering into Szohr's ear and cracking jokes with her.'

As it became apparent that they were indeed an item, details of how they first got together also started to seep out. It seems that the two became friends on set at first but then that platonic relationship evolved into something deeper. Soon Jessica was phoning Ed to ask him advice about boyfriends! He supposedly turned to her for relationship advice too, only for both of them to begin realising they had a lot in common and were becoming attracted to each other. Knowing when this friendship had turned into love was a difficult observation but Ed has talked about how he personally feels the emotions change: 'It's just that feeling and it's so hard to describe. It's when you give a f**k. You care what they think and how they feel. And then when you're not looking at anyone else, that's when you know she's The One.'

Of course, dating a fellow actor and being seen out in the Big Apple while you are both working on a very famous show that revolves around the relationships and lives of beautiful people in New York meant that there was always the risk that media intrusion into their relationship would be high. Talking to various magazines, Jessica admitted that it could be tricky sometimes: 'It can be a little awkward,' she told *Teen Vogue*, 'when all of a sudden [you have feelings for] someone you'd call to talk about a different boyfriend. But there wasn't a lot of thinking and talking. It kind of just happened. We had fun together, and we were like, "All right, let's see where this goes."' It also seems that the need for fun was a mutually enjoyed aspect of their relationship: 'He's a really rad guy. He's awesome and smart and talented and adorable, and we make each other laugh.'

It wasn't just having a laugh that the two seemed to be keen on. According to some reports, Ed is a dab hand in the kitchen (perhaps it's all that 'research' he does at fine restaurants!) and so although Jessica had been a vegetarian for over ten years since she'd quit eating meat as a teenager, he convinced her to try some of his home-cooking and it was so good, she started to eat meat again! 'After ten years of eating vegetarian, I tried my boyfriend's (food). I was overwhelmed. It was orgasmic!'

Of course, when it comes to special events, Ed and Jessica were quick to party! For Ed's 22nd birthday in March 2009, they headed out on the town with a bunch of friends – including *Gossip Girl* co-star Blake Lively – to New York's Lucky Strike Lanes and Lounge bowling alley, like millions of early twenty-somethings would do. However, this was not your usual bunch of twenty-somethings so inevitably the tabloids sources were observing. 'A guest' was quoted as saying, 'Ed and Jessica were close and cuddly all night. Everyone was friendly, having a lot of fun and were in good spirits.' The pals then tucked into home-made cupcakes topped with cookie dough, sweets, peanut butter, sprinkles and with the initials of 'HB ED' piped in icing on top before Ed blew out a lone candle and gave an impromptu, fun speech. 'Everyone sang "Happy Birthday", Ed thanked everyone for coming and kissed Jessica – they were adorable. Everyone bowled casually throughout the night, but no one really finished a game.'

Afterwards they partied on late into the night dancing to songs by bands such as the Kings of Leon and Notorious B.I.G.

In a cover feature for *Teen Vogue* in 2009, Jessica's down-to-earth personality was in full view during an interview in which she talked openly about her relationship with Ed. Not surprisingly, as successful actors and actresses, they sometimes love to splash the cash – for example, for Valentine's Day 2009 she and Ed went to Jamaica with Leighton Meester and her boyfriend, Sebastian Stan, a real *Gossip Girl* vacation! However, she revealed that they also like to keep it simple too, and love to 'go to dinners, have nights by ourselves and fun romantic times in general. And I like just cuddling up on the couch.' She is equally relaxed about her fashion too – the former child model is a fan of casual clothes, often wearing jeans and sweaters and walks around without much make-up – perhaps easier to do when you are so naturally beautiful!

Then suddenly, in April 2010, rumours began circulating on the Internet that the celebrity couple had split. Initially these rumours were angrily denied and paparazzi photos of the two out shopping for iPads seemed to dismiss the speculation. The media interest in their relationship seemed to somehow go up a notch when the split talk began, so Ed and Jessica found themselves followed pretty much every time they stepped out of the door.

One very glitzy event that Ed was photographed at during this time (he loves his glitzy events!) was the St Regis

International Cup at Cowdray Park in Sussex, a polo event that sees some of the wealthiest and most high-profile business people and celebrities in attendance. Afternoon tea was being served by staff from the five-star Lanesborough hotel and Tattinger champagne was chilled constantly for guests such as Jodie Kidd and Stereophonics' Kelly Jones, as well as a host of upper-class Brits. However, the paps' lenses all seemed to be aimed at Ed and there were quite a few journalists in attendance who were keen to talk to him. Wearing an Acne Breton T-shirt, Opening Ceremony shoes with J Crew jeans and hat, he was looking every bit the stylish Continental, but was honest enough to say, 'I've got no idea what [polo] is all about,' as he watched England beat South Africa. Then Ed was asked directly by one reporter about his girlfriend. 'No comment,' he said, 'It's a bit of a sore point and we're not together any more.'

Rumours started to circulate that Jessica was not only no longer with Ed but allegedly had moved on and was with another of her co-stars, namely Sebastian Stan, Leighton Meester's ex-boyfriend. This was strongly denied by both parties. There was talk that Ed and Jessica had had a big argument after her birthday party in Los Angeles where it was suggested she partied with her friends while Ed was away filming in the UK. Unsubstantiated rumours said Ed was furious to hear she had been 'flirting' with other men at the party and allegedly ended the romance during a mobile phone call from England. Supposedly, Jessica was so upset that she caught a cab straight to the airport and flew to the UK to be reunited with him. All rubbish, said her rep, 'The story has no merit.' The detail in this report finely illustrates the media and public fascination with their relationship and is a reminder of just how big *Gossip Girl* had become by this point. Together or not, Jessica and Ed were now in the full glare of the world's media.

Yet more unconfirmed reports suggested that Ed was hooking up with *90210* beauty AnnaLynne McCord, again denied. The rumour mill was now in full swing. That said, reading that particular report in full, it's easy to read between the lines and see that this was clearly just gossip – he was seen 'partying' with AnnaLynne but actually what was reported was the two chatting at a Prada event, before heading off to the *Express* and *Vogue* party together, during which 'he blew her a kiss at one point, and everyone in the room saw.' Another celeb who was 'linked' to Ed at this point was movie star Drew Barrymore, after being spotted out on the town with him at a Kings of Leon gig. An 'eyewitness' source told USWeekly.com that, 'Drew was hanging all over Ed. There was definite chemistry.' Both parties strongly denied there was any relationship.

Ed and Jessica's every movement was now being followed. The *New York Post* pointed out that the high-profile couple had sat separately at a Knicks game in mid-December, with Ed sitting under the basket with a male friend while Jessica sat centre-court with a girlfriend. Later the same evening,

Westwick was spotted at a restaurant with 'a mystery blonde'. After whispers and deep eye contact, 'the two left the table together and didn't return. A rep for Westwick didn't get back to us.'

Then, in classic *Gossip Girl* style, rumours began circulating that the couple were back together again! In July the couple were seen being very friendly in a Chicago hotel; according to the *New York Daily News*, a guest in the hotel's bar saw them merrily drinking shots together: 'They're definitely a couple. They were kissing and holding hands.' There were also photos of the two kissing and being very close at the US Tennis Open, which is hardly the place to have a secret liaison! A public kiss was caught by dozens of photographers while they watched Andy Roddick's 3–1 defeat by Serbian Janko Tipsarevic. Yet confusingly, news filtered back soon after that Ed had 'slammed reports' about any such reconciliation. And he tried to deflect the story by pointing out other beautiful actresses he was fond of: 'I'm single! My English accent drives American girls crazy but I haven't got time for romance. I've always been in love with Rachel Weisz, but sadly she's taken.' (And, for the record, she's English so the accent might not have such a hypnotic effect!)

By now, both Ed and Jessica were truly in the eye of a media storm and the magazines and newspapers ran stories on almost every aspect of their lives. Of course, such fame sometimes brings a negative side such as when reports surfaced alleging that the couple had failed to turn up to a promotional event, something that was vehemently denied by both their representatives. The story surrounded a period when they were staying at the Hard Rock Hotel in Chicago, where they were reportedly scheduled to make a public appearance. According to quotes from 'organisers', they were flown in first-class and given VIP tickets to the Lollapalooza festival; a report in the *New York Post* alleged that they stayed in their hotel rooms and ran up an $830 bill instead. The invite had been extended to Jessica and Ed was her so-called '+1' (that's a mightily impressive +1!). An argument was said to have ensued with publicists before they left, although the report did also make it clear that 'Jessica paid for everything.' However, representatives for both the stars completely refuted all of this and insisted the pair were not aware of any obligation to appear. Indeed, they said that as soon as Jessica found out – on the Sunday – about the issue, 'she agreed to pay for everything herself and left. There was no fight.' Ed's rep was in total agreement: 'Ed went as Jessica's +1 and had no idea about any agreement or photographs he had to take. He always honours any agreements.' It's worth pointing out that Ed has a strong reputation for attending charity dinners and events, often at celebrity auctions where he almost always buys a lot of stuff and in the process donates very large sums of money to charity.

So their reps had dismissed this alleged incident, but the furore does serve to illustrate the intense media interest in their relationship and the extent to which their private lives were now being scrutinised. My personal favourite media intrusion into their relationship is the following quote which said they had been spotted, 'canoodling between the salad and filet mignon' at the Old Homestead Steakhouse.

Then in the spring of 2010, it was confirmed that Ed and Jessica had split up, this time permanently it seemed. Unsubstantiated reports suggested that Jessica had cheated on Ed with a close friend, allegations that she denied. Women's magazines the world over were appalled at the idea, with *Company* saying, 'According to reports across the pond, the unthinkable has just happened.' However, no one actually saw any cheating. According to reports, it was Ed who ended the relationship. It must be noted once again that Jessica firmly and strongly denied any of these allegations.

The two-year relationship may have ended in less-than-ideal circumstances but Ed was clearly gutted. Most people were very surprised too (because Ed and Jessica had seemed like a very happy couple), including Ed's friend and co-star Chace Crawford. He was close pals with both of them and was said to be very shocked at the news.

Jessica's own career was yet to take another twist when in the late spring of 2011 she was axed from *Gossip Girl*'s forthcoming fifth season. Taylor Momsen would also not feature in that season although the door was left open for both of their characters to return in guest slots should the storyline demand it. While Taylor had been suspended from the show after she'd repeatedly courted controversy with her rock and roll behaviour fronting her band the Pretty Reckless (including copious amounts of swearing and saucy onstage photographs) Jessica was a little more sedate and was leaving amicably with a big screen Hollywood acting career in mind. After this news broke, Jessica also announced that she was planning to study abroad and might also possibly move to LA and buy a new house there.

Of course, Ed and Jessica weren't the only couple that sprang out of the show. Leighton Meester has been repeatedly linked with Ed, although usually after shots of them kissing while filming their characters' latest parts leaked out on to the Internet. Meester and Sebastian Stan dated and their colleagues Blake Lively and Penn Badgley enjoyed a high-profile relationship for some time too. Speaking to *Tatler* in March 2011, Ed revealed he was not completely surprised that there were so many romances on set, which he pointed out was a perhaps inevitable consequence of putting so many young and very beautiful people together almost 24 hours a day, working in close quarters for several years! 'Everyone's dated each other, and then broken up, or whatever. It's natural that romance would blossom. Blossom and then wilt.'

In the aftermath of his split from Jessica, Ed says that he has grown up and matured. The frenzy of the initial explosion of *Gossip Girl* success has both calmed him down a little and acclimatised him to life in the spotlight, so he has recently been able to feel more calm himself. 'My twenties have been incredible, it's been exciting, man! I think this last year has really been a year where I've grown up a hell of a lot, you know, certain situations and things.' Asked in a *Tatler* interview if he was still a romantic he joked, 'At the moment that's died a death, I'm kind of on the war path! The wickedness of women! God damn them!' Continuing in a more serious note he said, 'I've learned, I feel stronger and more wise. I'm only 23! How wise can I be?'

CHAPTER 9

The Fame Game

SEASON 4 SHOWED NO signs of Chuck Bass's role in *Gossip Girl* declining, which was obviously great news for Ed's career. Millions tuned in to see if the gun shot wound he'd suffered in the back streets of Prague had proved fatal. Fortunately it had not and a collective sigh of relief from Ed and Chuck fans around the world could almost be heard. However, Chuck seizes the opportunity to distance himself from the New York life he has come to detest in many ways and takes on a false alias – a literal and emotional distance from the old Chuck Bass that he now seems ashamed of. When he eventually arrives back in NYC with a Czech girlfriend, the Chuck–Blair dilemma is rekindled again, albeit this time with mostly negative and fiery arguments and scheming behind each other's backs. Over the season, Chuck seems to slip back into his bad guy lifestyle which almost seems a shame after the endearing chinks of light we had recently seen. He and Blair reunite then break up again as their on-off relationship reaches new heights of instability. After saving Blair from a kidnapper, the star-crossed lovers go to a bar mitzvah – how very *Gossip Girl*. The season ends with speculation that Blair might be pregnant with Chuck's baby. Once again, Ed's character is at the very heart of the season's meatiest storylines!

Back in the considerably less chaotic world of Ed Westwick, it wasn't just his own personal relationship that was under the spotlight – almost any aspect of his private life was seen as of interest to the media. Given his high profile, Ed's ability to enjoy a trouble-free night out in Manhattan was becoming increasingly limited! He makes no secret of the fact he enjoys a party with his friends and his nights out with Chace Crawford are the stuff of *Gossip Girl* legend. Ed is also a known restaurant connoisseur, and frequents many of the Big Apple's finest establishments. He was once asked what a perfect date would be and he replied 'Going out to dinner etc. etc., as long as it's expensive!'

Sometimes, however, events can unintentionally lead to headlines that he and his fellow cast members could probably do without. In January 2010, for example, Ed and his on-screen love interest Leighton Meester were out on the town together in NYC. Dining out at the super-posh Manhattan restaurant East 60th Street with their friends, newspapers alleged that they caused a 'big scene'. Media fingers were pointed at Meester, saying that after swearing loudly while other diners tried to eat in peace, she was asked to tone down her language only to reply, 'F**k you! How dare you tell us to keep it down.' Ed was clearly in a placatory mood if reports are to be believed, and went to chat to the diner who had taken offence. According to reports, he spoke gently with him and said, 'Don't worry about my friends. We should all be happy. Let's hug it up, guys!' and then gave the unsuspecting restaurant-goer a hug! Well done, Ed!

There are of course always two sides to every tale and many of the reports about celebrities are strongly denied by the stars. It's perhaps very easy to see why such a celebrity pairing caused a stir in New York though! With millions of *Gossip Girl* fans around the world, and probably several hundred thousand in NYC alone, the sight of the show's King and Queen of romance/relationships eating out together may well have been just too much for even the most shy of fans! Thank God Chace Crawford wasn't with them, the police might have been called!

Later in 2010, further reports suggested Ed became embroiled in another difficult night out in the city. Reporters claimed that Ed was enjoying a night out at the equally posh restaurant Los Feliz with friends when there were camera flashes at a nearby table. Reports said he became annoyed, and 'berated' the man for taking pictures of him, only for the diner to say he was simply taking photos of his own night out and didn't know who Ed was. Cruel reports suggested this annoyed Ed even more and, according to the *New York Daily*

News matters became even more heated. 'Ed came over and was like, "Stop taking my picture!" He started shouting obscenities at me and getting in my face. He was all bitter and s**t. I thought it was a joke. He walked off in a cloud of disgust. I went over to him and asked him who he thought he was, and he dissolved into a fit of rage.' Further reports claimed Ed asked for the man to be removed from the restaurant, suspecting he was a member of the paparazzi. Again when asked about the alleged incident, Ed's representative was dismissive, simply saying that 'there was no altercation'.

It wasn't just alleged incidents out on the town that sometimes attracted negative headlines for the stars of *Gossip Girl*. With any big TV hit, there will always be criticism. It's impossible to please everybody and *Gossip Girl* was not immune to this problem. So by Season 3's end, with ratings up and the PR presence of the show and its lead actors and actresses never higher, there was something of a backlash against the glamorous programme. The criticism and controversy came on several levels.

Some viewers objected to what they deemed an oversexualisation of teenagers. While the sexual intrigue is part of what the fans love about the show, it was inevitable it would draw criticism from older, or more conservative quarters.

Although much of the criticism about domineering males was directed at Chuck Bass, Chace's own character was not immune. People scoffed at the apparently materialistic obsessions of the lead roles and derided the superficial ambitions and lack of morals of many of the key faces from the show's characters. The show itself seemed confident that these criticisms were unduly harsh and so when one writer called it 'a parent's worst nightmare' *Gossip Girl* – they simply turned this around and made it a slogan for a new set of adverts. Critics cried foul, saying they were not taking their influence seriously.

Chuck Bass's part in this negativity was very prominent. His character is obviously the 'bad guy' of the show and at times his behaviour seems to know very few moral boundaries or depths to which he will not go. In particular, Chuck's relationship with Blair came under scrutiny. Chuck's darkness seems at times limitless and this has led some commentators to suggest that his relationship with Blair is in fact an abusive one (a feeling that increases most obviously throughout Season 4). This is perhaps the most controversial aspect of Ed's role. Of course, Chuck has done some fairly dirty deeds in the show, but it was a scene in Season 4 that stoked a raging controversy about how 'bad' his character was and also whether *Gossip Girl* had overstepped the mark.

During a row with Blair, Chuck threw a punch seemingly at her face, which missed but as his hand smashed a window behind her, glass fragments flew out and cut her cheek. This was presented almost as a sign of Chuck's love for Blair, in that his passion was so intense he had lost control; however, this caused an awful lot of consternation in the wider media. Many critics condemned the scene for supposedly glorifying domestic violence with Jezebel.com referring to Bass as a 'textbook abuser'. Some said it was made worse by the fact that Chuck was in fact a bad boy that many fans secretly adored. In an excellent article for FoxNews.com, journalist Hollie McKay put this controversial scene in context: 'According to Melissa Henson, Director of Communications and Public Education for the Parents Television Council, Hollywood has a dangerous habit of implying that these volatile relationships are more intense, more passionate than your average, run-of-the-mill romance.'

The accusation was that such scenes like this one from *Gossip Girl* 'romanticised' the violence, when in fact away from the glamour of the screen such aggression was simply terrifying. 'Today, the hidden message in the entertainment consumed by many impressionable teens,' continued Henson, 'is that if he hits you, it is out of love – which is absolutely wrong.' Of course *Gossip Girl* was not the first teenage drama to attract such accusations. Only recently the worldwide smash *Twilight* franchise was also harshly lambasted for the same problem, in that case hugely overpowering or controlling partners. Critics were fearful that watching shows such as *Gossip Girl* and *Twilight*, and seeing such 'abuse' on a regular basis might lead to that behaviour becoming accepted:

'Repeated and normalised views of this behaviour,' clinical psychologist Dr Jordana Mansbacher was quoted as saying, 'may cause desensitisation to this topic and can cause someone to find that they are in fact in an abusive situation when they were not aware they were even in one.' Executives behind *Gossip Girl* were moved to defend the scene, saying Chuck was most definitely not an abusive partner. Nonetheless, the Internet was soon littered with articles which screamed, 'Has *Gossip Girl* gone too far?'

Ed was inevitably asked about the behaviour of his character and of course said he was repulsed by any violence towards women. That was a given. Nonetheless, the controversy that this 'smashed glass' scene attracted added to the growing weight of criticism fired towards *Gossip Girl* for being too 'adult' when it was knowingly targeting a fan base of teens. This was not Ed's fault or concern of course, although as one of the most high-profile stars of the show and a regular promoter of *Gossip Girl* in the media and interviews on TV, he was always going to be asked about this hot topic. For him to then win Choice TV's 'Villain of the Year' award perhaps surprisingly worried the more conservative parents out there even more. In the same awards ceremony, *Gossip Girl* won 'Best TV Show Drama' and 'Best Breakout Show', while stars such as Blake Lively and Chace Crawford won gongs too. This reflected the enormous impact that *Gossip Girl* had had on this demograph. However, Ed thinks that these criticisms are overemphasised: 'Television heightens reality but I think *Gossip*

Girl comes very close,' he told the *Daily Mail*. 'The issues we deal with are universal: family; marriage; remarriage; parental approval; experimenting with drink and drugs … It's not a million miles from home and Britain's binge culture. But the programme is responsible. It shows the consequences of the negative side of life.'

Unfortunately, on occasion the criticism against Ed got personal. In the spring of 2009, Peaches, the daughter of Sir Bob Geldof, launched a scathing attack on Ed following a chance meeting with him, when she was quoted in *Grazia* as saying,

> 'He acts up to this personification of some sort of Pete Doherty character – some really wasted English guy with a poet soul and it doesn't really work. It is a bit like, "Mate, you're on *Gossip Girl* and you're in a sh**ty band." We spoke for a bit and he was quite lecherous. But he was lecherous to all the girls. He's very small, too. Smaller than me. I'm 5'7" and I think he must be 5'6". He's ripped [has muscles]. But when you're small and ripped you get into Tom Cruise territory, like a little overgrown gorilla.'

She also implied he overemphasises his English accent to impress American women. Not nice! Inevitably, you can only be the hottest 'new' show for a very small window of time and sure enough *Gossip Girl* soon found itself competing with the latest batch of great new programmes, such as *Grey's Anatomy* spin-off *Private Practice* and *Criminal Minds*. Other critics said the ratings weren't actually as high as people thought and that as yet the show had not translated overseas as well as predecessors such as *The OC*.

Another negative *Gossip Girl* rumour that the cast repeatedly denied was that certain members of the team hated each other and that on-set bitching and arguing was rife. This was largely another case of people confusing life with art but it was also an angle that the media and public alike found very titillating. As a result, Ed was constantly asked about it in interviews and he remained patient and diplomatic with his answers.

His ex-girlfriend Jessica Szohr was also frequently asked about any such on-set tensions and her answer speaks for the rest of the crew: 'I've heard horror stories from other actors about egos, people who don't get along, but we're all friends. There are people from this job who will be in my life for a very, very long time.' Ed concurred and was at pains to point to how well everyone got along: 'I learn so much every day, every week, every episode. And everyone on the show has created this great bond. We're like a family.'

Yet other quotes from stars of the show seemed to back up this rumour of tension on set. Fans of *Gossip Girl* would have gone into a rumour frenzy had they spotted any of the cast-couples double-dating but Penn Badgley was quick to dampen down any such suggestions, at the same time fuelling the speculation that sometimes it was not all as cosy on set as some of the crew would have you believe. Responding to the *New York Post*'s enquiry as to whether he and Blake Lively would go out with Ed and Jessica when they had reunited, he said, 'We're not friends. I mean, we just don't double date.'

Regardless of the extent of rumours about his private life, his co-stars, his nightlife, the good, the bad and the ugly of *Gossip Girl*, the swirling controversy around the show served to guarantee one thing above all else: that the programme, and therefore by definition Ed Westwick, became more famous than ever. Ed's fans are media savvy enough to know that his reputation as a nice guy (unlike Chuck!) is founded on facts rather than rumour and his name within Hollywood is as one of the most amenable and charming new actors in the world.

CHAPTER 10

Snow Storms, Bikinis and Mobile Phones

CONTINUING WITH ED'S RELENTLESS work schedule – bear in mind all his film appearances are in addition to his frantic work on the set of *Gossip Girl* – next up he filmed a very innovative short movie with none other than *Baywatch* legend and Hollywood sex siren Pamela Anderson. The film was a very intriguing and ultra-modern project that Ed was attached to in 2010 called *The Commuter*. The short film was a commercial marketing project that was to create a story to be shot entirely in high definition on a Nokia N8 mobile phone. Starring alongside Ed and Pammie were Dev Patel from *Slumdog Millionaire* and the revered stage and screen actor Charles Dance. The short was filmed in London so Ed was very much back on home turf!

The story follows Patel's character as he struggles to get to his first day at a new job; initially his car is clamped then he apparently misses the bus ... but then the film gets rather surreal as Patel starts to hallucinate. First up he fantasises that a nearby parking warden is in fact trying to kill him with a machine gun. He then fights a besuited ninja in China Town before escaping on to the London rooftops. Fights with violent bankers ensue as a chase scene sees Patel's commuter running for his life. Falling off a roof in desperation, he bizarrely ends up in Pamela Anderson's hotel room as the short film takes an even more peculiar twist. 'Sorry, I'm late for work,' he says before getting into a lift where the bellboy is one … Ed Westwick. Ed is on-screen for only a few seconds and his dialogue is restricted to just a few words. The bellboy's outfit is hardly his most fetching fashion statement either! Patel's commuter meanwhile runs off and steals a sports car, still desperate to get to work. At the end of the film, it is revealed that Patel is in fact still waiting at the bus stop and the whole sequence has been a daydream.

The role of 'bellboy in lift' seems a strange choice for Ed to make at this stage of his career, particularly as it was for a phone marketing campaign. Still, he got to work with Pammie Anderson and this was a real bonus as Ed had grown up watching those famous swimsuit sequences in *Baywatch*! Speaking about the short film, Ed said he felt 'like Sting in *Quadrophenia*' when shooting his scene! Certainly watching him shoot his meagre few lines in a poky lift doesn't exactly seem to reflect his massive popularity on *Gossip Girl*! Ed said, 'It's unique, you think about using a phone but it has the feel of a film set and has the same quality!' It was perhaps Ed's most bizarre choice of project to date.

Fortunately, not long after *The Commuter*, Ed returned to form with a lead role as Jonny in a high-profile romantic comedy called *Chalet Girl*, described by industry pundits as a 'teen Britflick'. Starring opposite Ed was the beautiful Felicity Jones; Felicity had previously been best known for voicing the character of Emma Carter on the world's longest running radio drama, *The Archers* on BBC Radio 4 and she had also impressed in various performances for the Royal Court Theatre, but nonetheless her casting in the movie's lead role was a big moment. *Chalet Girl* was a romantic comedy similar to *Bridget Jones* and *Pretty Woman* and given what those movies had done to the careers of Julia Roberts and Renée Zellweger, this was a great opportunity. Notably, although being 27 in real life, Felicity's character in the film is still a teenager!

Ed/Jonny's mother was the beautiful Brooke Shields and his father was played by the ever-hilarious Bill Nighy. Ed has since said that Bill made him laugh till he cried on set! Ed's adopted team of Chelsea are the sworn enemy of Bill's Manchester United so much of the on-set banter revolved around whose football team was best.

Ed had been sent the script and he loved what he read; fortunately the scheduling of the movie also fitted in perfectly with one of the very few breaks he gets from the hectic filming for *Gossip Girl*. He later found out that over 120 different versions of the script for *Chalet Girl* had been drafted so it was clear why the final version was so good!

The fact it was such a different genre to *Gossip Girl* appealed to Ed, even though like Chuck Bass, his character in the movie is very rich (although as a successful businessman Jonny has rather more to be financially proud of than Chuck!). Ed was also not afraid to admit that the idea of filming in the Alpine mountains of Germany and Austria (the film is set on the slopes of St Anton) appealed to him too! As a kid Ed had gone on annual school skiing trips from the age of 11 so he was a very capable skier. That said, the snowboarding sequences that form much of the storyline were a real challenge for him as he'd never tried this discipline before, so once he got to the film set he had some practice to do! 'It's such a picturesque location and the fresh air in your lungs, so yeah, all of those factors together, it was a definite [attraction].' Ed would eventually do all but one of the skiing scenes, with only one particularly difficult and risky jump left to a professional stunt skier. He had it a lot easier than Felicity though, as she had never skied on snow in her life, having only ever had a brief trip to a dry ski slope in the UK as a kid. She had to train for six hours a day for four weeks to get ready for the shoot.

Ed did say however that some of the filming was very difficult because the sunshine bouncing off the snow was so bright that the cast were dazzled and most of them spent long hours squinting at each other. One more sinister moment came when filming was halted after a severe snow storm led to the slopes being completely evacuated.

The atmosphere on set was very jovial, even though Ed had not previously worked with any of his co-stars. The crew and cast were predominantly English and 'we had mutual friends,' he told *ViewLondon*, 'so I felt like we kind of knew each other anyway. It was a great experience in that respect, that we all kind of bonded together really quickly. That's a perfect situation when you're working on a film, especially when you're away from friends and family as well and you're with the people you're working with – afterwards you have dinner and stuff like that, so it was great.'

There were quite a few laughs on set too, with one particular scene where the characters play a game called 'Ibble Dibble' with corks on their heads but the cast kept cracking up laughing. The same fit of giggles grabbed Ed when another character walked past him and said, 'Awesome sauna, bro', and no one could stop laughing every time he said it! The genuine camaraderie was clear and Ed especially got on well with Nick Bran, who plays his on-screen brother-in-law.

Ed's character Jonny is a warm-hearted, very wealthy young man who on the surface appears to have everything a guy could want: a beautiful fiancée, a great job, lots of money and so on. However, he hankers after something different, there is an ache inside him that nags at him to enjoy life more. It is while Jonny is holidaying at his parents' ultra-swanky Alpine chalet – reminiscent of Chuck's lifestyle perhaps? – that he meets the poor chalet girl of the film's title. This unassuming chalet cleaner is actually a former snowboarding champion and prodigy called Kim whose own promising career was cut short by the death of her mother, so she shares a sense of being unfulfilled with Ed's character. Kim is initially working at a burger bar but the opportunity arises to work on the slopes as a chalet cleaner and she grabs it with both hands – although she hardly fits the posh chalet girl stereotype. In the film, a snowboard tournament gives her the opportunity to reignite that passion for the slopes and discover a new passion ... for Ed/Jonny!

During the promotion of the film, Ed shot a cover feature for the highly influential fashion and lifestyle magazine *Tatler* alongside co-star Felicity Jones. In the article, he revealed it was a refreshing change to play someone who wasn't as evil as Chuck! '[I'm] playing someone who's a bit more like I am – a nice boy! He has a heart, he has a soul, and he's still figuring out his place in the world.' Ed was also drawn to the English comedy in the film, as he was a childhood fan of the *Carry On* movies and also loved great British comedy writers such as Richard Curtis, Ben Elton and Rowan Atkinson.

Ed and Felicity clearly got along very well and so too did the rest of the crew from the film. One of the more fun anecdotes from this promotional time was the headline about Ed and his on-set pals 'drunkenly skiing' in search of a bar! They were shooting in St Anton, Austria, and Tamsin Eggerton, who also appears in the movie, explained to *Bang Showbiz* what happened:

'We went to the Krazy Kangaroo bar and we had a few Jägermeisters too many and we didn't know how to get down the slope to the next bar. So Ed just got on his back and "skied" all the way down and everyone was like, "Ooh!" and then the other guys said, "That's really cool, I want to do that!" We all just kind of piled out, fell on top of each other at the end and then went back into the bar.'

Felicity Jones was also very warm in her praise of Ed and made an entire generation of *Gossip Girl* fans jealous with this revelation: 'Ed is an excellent person to get to know and he made the whole thing very easy and relaxed. And from his years of training on *Gossip Girl* he really knows how to be on set and he's really incredible professional ... [and] ... he is a very good kisser.'

Ed also felt he learnt from the director of *Chalet Girl*, Phil Traill. Phil had previously directed such films as *All About Steve* and TV hits such as *10 Things I Hate About You* and *Cougar Town*. 'Phil was great,' said Ed. 'Very relaxed approach, made you feel very comfortable. One of the gang, definitely. Obviously when I saw the film I was really pleased with what he'd done and especially one of the key elements in the film, the soundtrack, which was very appropriate for the film and raised the atmosphere tenfold. It's an absolutely great choice, so I'm very pleased with what he did.'

The film received only mixed reviews on its release in March 2011. It was premiered at the Westfield cinema in west London on 8 February 2011 and not surprisingly hundreds of Ed and *Gossip Girl* fans turned up!

In the main, Felicity Jones received the highest praise but there were some doubters too. Tim Robey writing for the *Daily Telegraph* said the film 'keeps threatening to sink into a squishy mulch of inadequately scripted formula'. He also said Ed's character was 'goofy'. The *Chicago Tribune* said it was 'an obvious crowd-pleaser that relies too heavily on staged, sitcom-style humour and stereotypical characters that not even Bill Nighy and Brooke Shields can save'. The *Daily Mirror* was more generous saying it was 'a fun-packed affair' while the *Guardian* was also (surprisingly) impressed, noting it was 'Amiable, silly, feel-good stuff, destined to do nicely'.

However, despite some critics being less than kind, the film was the highest new entry in its first week of release with nearly £700,000 in takings in just five days; it was fourth in the top ten films, which was topped that week by Johnny Depp's CGI blockbuster *Rango*. An Oscar-winning film it may not have been but *Chalet Girl* was another notch on Ed's film portfolio and did at least extend the type of roles that he might be offered in the future.

This fact seems to be confirmed by two roles which Ed is working on at the time of writing. Firstly, he is attached to a biopic of FBI head honcho J Edgar Hoover, a project that has potential to be exactly the sort of highly credible critics' favourite that Ed is so keen to be involved with. For starters, the movie is being directed by the genuine Hollywood legend,

Clint Eastwood. Further, the lead in the movie is played by Leonardo DiCaprio, an actor whom Ed has made no secret of admiring and aspiring to follow in terms of his career. Ed's role in *J Edgar* is that of a special operative who has a unique writing skill and is asked by Hoover to work with him on his biography. The film will also star Armie Hammer who had herself been on *Gossip Girl* a few years previously. *J Edgar* started filming in February 2011 and is due to hit cinemas some time in 2012.

A second undoubtedly credible move for Ed is a role in the forthcoming film adaptation of the classic Shakespeare tale, *Romeo and Juliet*. In the early summer of 2011 it was reported that Ed was in 'final negotiations' to appear as Tybalt in the new project, with Hailee Steinfeld as Juliet and Holly Hunter also attached to the movie. Although Ed isn't lined up as the main love interest of Juliet, her cousin Tybalt is in fact the play's main antagonist who is eventually killed by Romeo. It's a demanding and high-profile part, previously played in other adaptations by such revered actors as John Leguizamo and the brilliant Alan Rickman. Filming under the director Carlo Carlei is penned in to start in Verona in the summer of 2011 with a release date provisionally being later in 2012.

Ed was clearly very excited at the prospect: 'We got a really, really great script,' he told reporters in Manila. 'It's keeping the traditional flow of Shakespeare's traditional language but it was made a little bit more accessible to a contemporary generation. And yeah, it's going to be fantastic.'

CHAPTER 11

A Date With Chuck Bass

WITH ED'S FILM AND TV career being so high profile, there are lots of questions that interviewers and fans alike want to ask him. Of course, there are also other aspects of his life that the public want to know about that are not quite so career-oriented, perhaps the most obvious question being, 'Just what sort of girl would Ed Westwick like to date?'

Obviously Ed's ex-girlfriend Jessica Szohr is a beautiful and famous actress but he's also on record as saying he likes to be with a girl who makes him laugh. He admits he likes pretty girls but says this is not all he is attracted to: 'I've been attracted to girls [when] it is not about looks. You get that connection and sometimes it's totally involuntary.' And he's pointed out that he doesn't have a 'type' of girl that he always goes for.

With the emphasis on style and fashion being so heavy in *Gossip Girl* (more of that later!), it's no surprise that Ed likes a girl who knows how to dress. However, he also thinks that even the most beautiful clothes will not make him attracted to a girl if she has the wrong personality: 'As long as it's done the right way, I think it'll be attractive. It's not about what it is, it's about who's wearing it. From my limited knowledge of women's fashion, everything is pretty good.' So it's a combination of 'a good sense of style and confidence' that will win him over.

Ed's obviously a romantic too. 'I'm childish at times, passionate, a little crazy, I guess. And I pride myself on being one of the last romantics,' he once said. When asked what the grandest gesture he ever made to a girlfriend was, he replied, 'It sounds so clichéd but I scattered rose petals around a hotel room and ordered in some very, very expensive champagne. It was for a birthday, and we had a private party before the big birthday party.'

Despite his fame and money, and the fact that he can get into all the best clubs and restaurants in NYC, Ed's favourite way of spending time with a girl is in fact at home. 'The best thing about relationships? Cuddling on the couch and eating food in bed. Crumbs can come into the bed too, they're fine.'

In keeping with the texting/online slant of *Gossip Girl*, Ed's admitted to sending his girlfriends fruity text messages. The modern plague of so-called 'sexting' has seen the downfall of many celebrity relationships as tabloid newspapers have found out all about illicit affairs and flirting via such naughty messages. However, Ed reserves his cheeky texts strictly for his girlfriends. He says he likes to text his partner because it can often be easier than phoning, especially with his hectic schedule – if he is in between shots on set, there is usually no time, nor is it always appropriate for him to take a phone call but he can fire off a quick text to say hi. 'Oh yeah, I send saucy texts all the time,' he told *Bang Showbiz*. 'They're very saucy you know. I use that classic line, "What are you wearing?" People are braver when it comes to texts because they can hide behind them.'

Of course, his fans will try to send him saucy messages too but on one occasion this nearly backfired rather badly! While on a promotional tour for Virgin Mobile, Ed had amazingly given out his mobile number to some fans so that they could text him and, perhaps not surprisingly, the majority of the fan messages that came into his phone were pretty fresh. The problem was, many of them had misdialled and were actually sending very suggestive texts by mistake to the phone number of an entirely innocent married man. Unfortunately, his wife then saw these messages and assumed, quite understandably, that her husband was having an affair! The innocent man phoned Ed and told him the disastrous consequences and luckily Ed stepped in and explained the problem to the man's wife, then texted out his correct number to the same fans!

It's pretty certain that Ed probably doesn't need to use many chat-up lines these days, but he does admit to having used a few corny ones when he was younger and unknown. 'I'm not a "Get your coat, you've pulled" kind of guy. Although I'm sure I did use that line when I was 13 at the under-18s disco!' He's often made fun of his younger self's failure to attract girls, clearly something which is no longer a problem in his life. 'I was a 24/7 stud. It came effortlessly, girls were dripping off me …' he joked to *Bang Showbiz*. 'No, not at all! I'm joking. I was jealous of one of my friends at school because he was always dating the older, good-looking girls. That never happened to me.' Not any more, Ed! And if he did see a girl he fancied, he would obviously not be shy in coming forward: 'You have to have a degree of confidence. I'm not über-confident in that respect, but if you like someone you've got to go for it because if you don't ask, you'll never know.'

Although he has explained that he fell in love with Jessica over quite a long period of time, he doesn't think this is necessarily the only way to find a partner because he has said that he also believes in love at first sight. Talking to *Cosmopolitan* magazine he said that being in love 'is incredible, it's intoxicating. To fall in love with someone at first sight is fine, but in order to have a working relationship you need to realise that love is just one thing in a whole relationship.'

Although Ed's strong English accent comes across to American women as highly sophisticated, he's not averse to being a little bit saucy. Apparently he rarely turns up to work on the set of *Gossip Girl* wearing underpants, because he prefers the feeling of 'going commando'. Then if his role that day requires him to cover his modesty, he simply borrows new undercrackers that have been bought in for his character Chuck ... and then takes them home after filming! 'I show up without it and have to put it on. I don't usually wear underwear. It's more comfortable and free to air it all out.'

He also teased his millions of fans by saying he's never too tired to make love. 'Sleep or sex? Sex, man. Straight up. Sex, then sleep. I've got a great appetite for ... um, everything.' He also revealed that when he was a younger man he had once made out with a girl in public, although pointed out that it was 'not George Michael public'! He hinted that making out in public is something he might like to revisit with a woman! That comment must have set the pulses of thousands of 'cougars' all over Manhattan racing. Mind you, Ed is also on record as saying the most romantic place in Stevenage is 'my bedroom!'

So Ed seems quite confident when it comes to romancing and approaching women, yet when the conversation turns a little more serious, he is often coy when asked about who he has genuinely been in love with. When talking to *Bang Showbiz* he was noticeably reticent to name names. 'I've only been in love once – with my mum. There's only one woman in my life. Am I a mummy's boy? Absolutely. I love her.' As with many of his *Gossip Girl* co-stars, questions about his private life, especially any love interest, pepper any interview, to the extent that many journalists are now asked before each meeting to preferably not ask him if he is single or dating anyone. To Ed's credit, if the question is asked regardless, he always seems good-tempered about his answer; after his split from Jessica, for example, when he must have still been feeling sore, he told one writer that, 'Girlfriends are too much of a headache.' But the old romantic in him is never far from the surface: 'I'm all for being in love. And whenever I like someone, I end up pretty much completely smitten.'

Aside from his own celebrity girlfriends, Ed has revealed many a crush on other famous faces including Cheryl Cole and Rachel Weisz. Speaking of the media frenzy around Cheryl Cole, and also the number of men linked to her after her split from husband and footballer Ashley Cole, Ed joked, 'Everyone is obsessed with her right now so it's freaking me out. I think she needs to chill out, disappear and give me a call.' He pointed out that he loved Cheryl's soft Geordie accent which was a dialect he was very familiar with as his father hails from the north-east of England. And obviously, her incredible looks played a part, saying 'she just does it for me'. He pondered whether she should pursue a career in acting ... so that she could then land roles starring opposite him! 'I play a double agent and I'd love Cheryl to be in the film,' he told the *Daily Mirror*. 'Imagine that. Cheryl would be amazing. I'll have to speak to [a production team] to write her in ... Can you imagine Cheryl, my leading lady!' He wasn't alone in admiring the Girls Aloud star of course – along with most of the male Western world, a string of celebrities had declared their lust/love for her, including Olly Murs, Will.I.Am and even Chace Crawford! With such heavy competition, how would

Ed romance one of the world's most beautiful and desirable women? He said he'd take her out for fish and chips!

The second question that Ed Westwick inevitably gets asked in interviews and when he meets fans is simply how does he compare to his on-screen character Chuck Bass? Ed is asked about the similarities between himself and Chuck in almost every single interview he does, which must eventually get quite tiring! However, he will always try to provide an illuminating answer; take this one in the *Daily Mail*:

> 'Chuck is completely diabolical but he is quick-witted and not intimidated by anyone. He goes after what he wants. It's just the nature of what he wants which is not good. But there are a lot more differences than similarities between Chuck and me. When I was 17, I had certain characteristics of Chuck's, but obviously the context was different. I didn't come from the Upper East Side and I didn't have the same desires. Oh, and I didn't have a string of lovers. I'm a good boy.'

Having played Chuck Bass for so long, it's inevitable that Ed has developed an affection for the character he plays, even though Chuck can behave so badly. When asked by *Tatler* if spending several years of his life immersed in the mindset of a super-wealthy evil-doer had made him averse to such rich kids, he replied, 'No, not at all. I mean I wouldn't say I'm unsympathetic to individuals who are rich. A sense of emptiness might come from an idea of "Do I deserve this? Why me? What's my value?" … But I'm not empty, I'm definitely not empty.'

One area of his life where there is clearly no similarity with Chuck is the amoral values his character seems to ooze. 'My favourite dastardly Chuck Bass thing?' he told *Tatler*. 'It's got to be whoring Blair out to his uncle … ' He's also commented, '[The fans are] used to seeing this nasty side on TV, but that's not the real me. Chuck's a bad boy, and that's fun to play. But I would never manipulate someone for my own benefit.' If that is the case, how does Ed immerse himself in the dark character so convincingly? He says whenever he is playing Chuck on set, he dips into memories of arrogant and selfish people that he has met in person in his own life and those feelings and thoughts fuel his ability to create an ever more convincing Chuck.

But if Chuck is such a bad boy, why is he still so popular? 'People find the bad boy appealing – I guess it's a certain fantasy about things that a lot of us don't want to do. They are naughty and they are kind of bad.'

Ed has also denied that the party animal persona which Chuck boasts of and which the press like to give him too is accurate. Photos of him at many nightclubs around NYC, eating in fine restaurants with beautiful women and being spotted at numerous premieres, charity auctions, polo events and the like, led some magazines to suggest that the social lives of Ed and Chuck were perhaps more similar after all. Not so, he says: 'I'm not into scene-y spots, so we hang out in people's apartments. And I'd rather be known for my career than my whereabouts. To be respected as an actor it doesn't help to be seen out in the clubs.'

At the same time, it's clear that the fame surrounding Chuck Bass can unavoidably sometimes feel quite suffocating, as this quote from superiorpics.com suggests: 'If I want to go out and drink and throw a glass in the street, I'll do it as long as the reason is that I want to have fun and not that I want to create some sort of tension around me. Then I'd be a d**k, but I'm not.'

Like most *Gossip Girl* viewers, Ed's feelings towards Chuck have warmed over the seasons – remember, in the pilot episode Chuck attempted to rape, or at least sexually assault both Serena and Jenny. However, in subsequent episodes the writers seemed to dilute this sinister edge a little: 'I think I share the opinion of my character that a lot of the audience shares,' he told superiorpics.com. 'It's a love to hate kind of thing. As the seasons progressed, I think everyone's had sympathy for him. I think he's an alluring character. He's very interesting. He has these slices of his personality. He can be the devil, but at times he can be very charming. It can be a very dangerous concoction. I think he has a good heart, but his heart is often tempted by corrupt desires.'

One obvious difference between Chuck and Ed is the accent. The contrast between Ed's natural London accent and that of

Chuck Bass is quite extreme, yet Ed has never had any dialect coaching or professional tutoring to achieve the impressive vocal trickery. He explains that he simply listens intently to people speaking in a certain way and insists that the careful control of his tongue and recalling these people's accents enables him to achieve Chuck's extremely convincing US accent flawlessly.

So convincing was Ed's American accent in *Gossip Girl* that when fans of the show started to scout around the Internet for his previous work, many of them remained oblivious to his roots, with several online forums laughing at his 'fake British accent' in earlier shows like *Casualty* and *Doctors*.

Much of the time, Ed actually finds himself explaining away his nationality: 'A lot of people still don't realise I'm English, which is funny. The amount of times I've said, "Yes, I'm English."' By contrast, a lot of women who do know use this fact to hit on him: 'Some girls say the weirdest things like, "I've been to London", then they try to have a conversation with me all about London. I'm like, "Great!"'

One final comparison worth mentioning between Ed and Chuck is their differing senses of style! Within a few months of the first episode being screened, one aspect of *Gossip Girl*'s appeal that was almost as popular as Ed and his fellow actors was the style and fashion on show! This has become a crucial part of *Gossip Girl*'s success and of course Ed and Chuck were instrumental in this. Chuck is clearly the most outrageous member of the cast in terms of what he wears!

Chuck's signature fashion item is an expensive scarf, often checked, always loud! He wears his suits cut very tight and often quite short and complements these threads with exorbitantly expensive Italian leather shoes or luxurious boat shoes. Although he has been seen in basketball boots, he never wears trainers. Chuck is famously unafraid to wear colours (!) so we have seen him in sweaters that make a rainbow look dull, including lime greens, bright yellows, pinks and reds. He mixes up colours with patterns too, being fond of checks, herringbone, argyle, tartan and so on. Chuck's style is the modern perfection of a so-called 'preppy' look, and as each season of *Gossip Girl* came along, millions of men across the world tried to copy his fashion. Ed's character benefits from wearing a dazzling array of bespoke tailored garments and is therefore never anything but perfectly dressed; the problem is that this look is not a cheap one. Consequently a large number of style and fashion magazines have analysed Chuck's style and offered their readers advice on how to go about replicating the look!

Chuck's striking and at times frankly bizarre high-fashion styling is a stark contrast to Ed's earlier characters. He had started his career playing petty thieves and low income wannabes in films such as *Breaking and Entering* or dramas such as *Casualty*, but with his fame now assured through *Gossip Girl*, at times his wardrobe in real life was under the spotlight as much as his acting. The tabloids were quick to highlight the apparent blurring of the lines between fashion fact and fiction: 'Let loose from the confines of Chuck Bass suit-dom,' said IMDb.com, 'Mr Westwick opts for deep, nearly belly-button-baring V-necks and continues to be relentless with plaids we've never seen on a Scottish bagpiper ... While it'd seemingly be a good idea for Ed to take a cue from his more polished *Gossip Girl* character, his new-found affinity for ascots may prove otherwise.'

It is ironic that Ed's fashion has moved towards Chuck's in this way, given that his own personal style has previously always been much more of a rock and roll look, akin to that of the UK rocker Pete Doherty from the Libertines (the band that the Filthy Youth were frequently compared to). With Ed being photographed out at many premieres and charity functions, the majority of the mainstream photos of him are inevitably in more formal clothes; however, he still loves to wear much more casual attire: 'Chuck is an iconic character and the clothes are iconic,' he told one reporter. 'I think I rock the look well. My style has always been good; top notch, baby. I like the glamorous indie rock look, like the Libertines. But you know, without the heroin needle sticking out of my arm.'

In fact Ed says one of his most obvious fashion influences is Johnny Depp and he refers back through the famous actor to the guitarist who inspires a lot of both of their wardrobes: the Rolling Stones' Keith Richards. 'I kind of like that rock and roll look.' Ed loves to wear skinny black jeans which he says accentuate his figure best of all and he is also, of course, famous for ripping the tops of his shirts so that they show that little bit of extra chest!

Ed credits *Gossip Girl* with teaching him a lot about fashion and admits that since he has appeared on the show his own style has vastly improved. 'My fashion consciousness – and self consciousness – have definitely grown over the course of being on the show,' he was quoted as saying by contactmusic.com. 'All the exposure and all the experience I've had of different sides of the industry means I have a better knack of how to put things together. We've all been to fashion shows, we've worked with designers in different capacities, on fashion shoots. You learn about different looks and colours. I've definitely stepped up my game.'

In sharp contrast to the 'chav' street looks of his earlier acting roles, Ed now has a growing interest in the 'English country gentleman' style: 'A grey flannelly wool-type trouser,' he told *Metro*, 'brown shoes – no socks, of course – white shirt, grey waistcoat. Chic but smart-casual, great for late summer, early autumn. I'm going to have to go out and grab that one … '

His improving fashion sense was recognised by the influential *GQ* magazine in the autumn of 2010 when they awarded him the 'Breakthrough Talent of the Year' gong. Mind you, if Ed is to maintain his recent status as one of the most stylish men on the planet he might have to finally overcome what he says is his worst habit – biting his fingernails! He refuses to have a manicure too, saying he is 'a man's man'!

With such a high profile, it was no surprise that Ed was soon being approached by some of the world's top brands to help them market their wares. The cool trainer company K-Swiss won his affection and he became the second *Gossip Girl* cast member to sign an endorsement deal, after Leighton Meester. All the cast are frequently given very large piles of free designer clothes, shoes, beauty products and so on, something which Ed is on record as saying is one of the best perks of the job! For any twenty-something interested in fashion and style, it's a fair point! But K-Swiss was something which really intrigued him because his own personal style is deeply rooted in street fashion. Consequently Ed has been seen in various parts of the globe promoting the footwear, signing autographs, helping launch new styles and meeting *Gossip Girl* fans.

There have been downsides to Ed being in such a focused fashion spotlight; in 2010, the tabloids rather harshly suggested that Ed had put on some weight and that the chiselled angular look of Chuck Bass was proving hard to keep up; there was even a rumour – denied of course – that producers of *Gossip Girl* were worried he might lose his stunning looks if he kept putting on weight. Shots of him filming in the summer of 2011 quickly dispelled these uncharitable rumours anyway, as Ed looked absolutely amazing!

As long as Ed continues to star in *Gossip Girl* he will be asked how he compares to his controversial yet much-loved character Chuck Bass. Perhaps the many obvious differences between Ed and Chuck are best left to the actor himself to sum up: 'We look the same, but that's about it.'

CHAPTER 12

The Future

ALTHOUGH *GOSSIP GIRL* SHOWS little sign of running out of steam any time soon and Ed also makes no secret of his love for the role that broke him, the career ambition that saw him get that job in the first place is now pushing him to widen his horizons. It is an entirely natural development that he is obviously thinking about life after Chuck Bass: 'It's all about the work, you know,' he told *Tatler*, 'the feeling you get when you connect to the work. And that's what I had with Chuck Bass in the beginning, I was fascinated by him. But now to be completely honest, I'm ready to do something else. *Really* ready to do something else.' In other interviews around the time of promoting *Chalet Girl* in 2010 he seemed to reiterate his eagerness to move on soon. Speaking to *Metro* in London – whose reporter called him 'ridiculously handsome' – he said, 'I'd like to not play a high-school kid any more,' I'd be up for doing some action but really, I'm open to anything … '

When these quotes were printed, *Gossip Girl* fans were dismayed and assumed Ed was literally about to leave the show, but he soon clarified to *OK!* *what* he had actually meant: 'That was kind of taken out of context. What I actually said was that I wanted to maximise my time, but I had agreed to do other projects as well. I'm having a fantastic time with *Gossip Girl*, (it's a) great character, great cast and I live in New York City.'

Nonetheless, *Gossip Girl* will not continue for ever, so Ed will eventually begin a new phase of his still young career. Amongst other things, 'something else' might include a return to his days with the Filthy Youth or at least a rock band somewhere in the world. He's also made no secret of his desire to spend some time in theatre, treading the boards in more serious productions. Having played roles on stage before his TV and movie career took off in his teens, Ed is keen for a return to the theatre at some point. He's also a lifelong fan of London's West End and a role in one of the big productions there would be a fabulous career high. In recent times, a string of big name stars have enjoyed – and been praised for – roles in the Theatreland of the capital's West End (Kim Cattrall, Daniel Radcliffe and Orlando Bloom for example). After years of playing a TV character on a closed set for millions of fans worldwide, it seems the physicality of a small theatre has a very definite appeal: '[I'd like] something intimate, so that people can get to know the real me – without a screen in the way.' Given his background in the Filthy Youth, Ed has also said he would love to win a part in a musical and give his vocal cords another chance to shine!

And, of course, his Hollywood movie career is still a priority, with a rumoured move to Los Angeles a perhaps inevitable next step. Ed has spoken openly of his love for the Batman franchise: 'It would be a dream come true to play Batman in a big blockbuster movie. He was my childhood superhero. He's a damn good fighter and has access to amazing gadgets, such as the utility belt and, of course, the Batmobile – I'd give my left arm just to sit in it.'

Ed's also mentioned an ambition to work with actor/director Gary Oldman and also the legend Francis Ford Coppola, so he clearly has very lofty aims. He cites his favourite film of all time as being the Coppola-directed *The Godfather* so that gives some indication of where his dream roles might lie.

Or maybe we won't see him in a major blockbuster movie after all? Why? Because he won't get the role? No! Because he was once asked what his dream job was and his answer was … a landscape gardener! Speaking in the media he said, 'I think gardens are fantastic and I'd love to draw and design and stuff like that. I love just planting flowers during the summer. There's something very humble about it and natural and beautiful. When I need to think of like a peaceful scene or something, I think of my back garden in summertime. And whenever I hear the lawnmower next door, I always think it's really peaceful.' He's also on record as saying that if he could swap jobs for a day with anyone, it wouldn't be another film star, or a rock star or even his favourite footballer David Beckham, but an Amazon explorer!

Perhaps other areas of the arts might draw him in? Remember that famous sketch of the Filthy Youth playing a New York gig back in 2008? In 2009 it was reported that Ed was collaborating on a 'secret' art project called 'Places to See' with the artist behind that sketch, one Todd DiCiurcio, as well as Richard Phillips.

And has all the fame and adulation gone to his head? Apparently not. Ed seems to have a very down-to-earth approach to his celebrity. Sometimes his fame still appears to catch him out. The success of *Gossip Girl* is now so worldwide that Ed is finding almost any international travel can come with a lot of attention. On a trip to Iceland, he was forced to stay longer than expected because of extreme winter conditions grounding flights. For him this caused extra security headaches because there were so many screaming fans! 'Beatlemania!' he told *Tatler*, 'I was like, "Leave me alone! This is silly!"'

And yet despite this worldwide celebrity, Ed is still clearly not thinking of himself as in the same realms as his own heroes. For example, Ed is a Queen's Park Rangers fan and also follows the fortunes of Chelsea, but it is the aforementioned former Manchester United star whom he most idolises – David Beckham (he had a Beckham Number 7 Manchester United shirt when he was a kid). Due to his own celebrity, Ed has twice found himself in the same room as his sporting hero, but on both occasions he has simply been too star-struck to approach the soccer legend. At a grand ball in

New York one evening where Beckham was sitting at the next table with George Clooney, Ed went to the bathroom only for Beckham to walk in, but the *Gossip Girl* star was dumbstruck by the soccer star's presence. 'I couldn't say anything,' he told *Reveal*. 'I just ran out. A friend tried to persuade me to say, "Hello", but I couldn't do it. It was ridiculous … There have been a couple of times now that I've been in the same room as him, but I just can't go up to him. I can't do it.'

Despite the fame, the money, the attention of millions of women around the world, the critical plaudits and the privileged lifestyle that he can now enjoy like his character Chuck Bass, Ed is not about to lose sight of the lad from Stevenage that dreamed of being an actor as a young kid. 'There are perks to this job,' he was quoted as saying in superiorpics.com. 'We [the *Gossip Girl* cast] were all thrown into this situation with a lot of attention on us and you get a lot of free clothes and s*** but that's no reason not to stay grounded. What am I really doing, baby? Saving the world? Nah, I'm on television.'

PICTURE CREDITS

Now flip the book to read all about Chace!